A Carer's Guide to Schizophrenia

Greg Wilkinson

Tony Kendrick

The ROYAL
SOCIETY *of*
MEDICINE
PRESS Limited

PUBLISHED WITH AN EDUCATIONAL GRANT FROM LILLY INDUSTRIES

1 Wimpole Street, London W1M 8AE, UK
16 East 69th Street, New York, NY 10021, USA

British Library Cataloguing in Publication Data

A catalogue record for this book is available from the British Library

ISBN 1-85315-298-6

Composition by Ken Brooks, Sawbridgeworth, Herts, UK

Printed in Great Britain by Finesse Print, Maidstone, Kent

Contents

1 What is schizophrenia?

Schizophrenia is a broad term used to describe a number of related serious mental illnesses, which tend to be severe and long-term. They are found in all cultures and affect one in 100 people at some time in their life. At any one time between three and four in every 1000 people experience problems associated with schizophrenia. The disease usually begins in adolescence or early adult life, generally about five years earlier in men than in

women. The earlier the illness begins, the worse the long-term consequences for leading a normal life tend to be.

After a first episode of schizophrenia there is a tendency for the illness to recur and for some degree of long-term disability to develop. A quarter of sufferers recover within five years, two-thirds show a fluctuating course over tens of years and one in ten develop an incapacitating long-term illness.

Schizophrenia is one of the most severe of the psychiatric disorders and, in spite of modern treatment methods and rehabilitation, remains a major source of personal distress and social difficulties. The stigma surrounding schizophrenia persists, such that it is often wrongly thought as being frequently associated with violence, though in reality most people with schizophrenia are not violent and most of any aggression is often directed towards themselves.

——— Symptoms of schizophrenia

There is no laboratory test for schizophrenia and the diagnosis is based on the patient's symptoms. These are divided into frightening positive symptoms, like hallucinations and delusions, and negative symptoms, such as blunted emotions, lack of interest and energy, apathy and social withdrawal. There are also distortions of thought processes and perception, and inappropriate moods.

No one symptom clinches the diagnosis but those that often occur together include:

A   Disturbances of thinking: eg. complaints of thoughts being inserted or withdrawn from the mind and of hearing thoughts broadcast aloud.
B   Delusions of being controlled (by electricity or unspecified powers), relating to body or limb movements or actions, or sensations.

C   Hallucinatory voices giving a running commentary on the person's behaviour or discussing the person among themselves, or coming from some part of the body.

D   Persistent delusions of other kinds that are inappropriate and impossible such as religious or political identity (being God or The President), or superhuman powers and abilities.

E   Persistent hallucinations accompanied by delusions when occurring for weeks or months on end.

F   Breaks in the train of thought, resulting in incoherent or irrelevant speech or use of made-up new words.

G   Catatonic behaviour such as excitement, strange posturing, becoming mute or in a stupor.

H   Negative symptoms such as apathy, poor speech and emotional responses, social withdrawal, and lowered social performance.

I   A significant and consistent change in personal behaviour shown as loss of interest, aimlessness, idleness or self-absorbed attitude and social withdrawal.

Adapted from ICD–10

People with schizophrenia may also suffer from symptoms of anxiety, depression, and other milder symptoms of emotional distress. An important aspect of schizophrenia is the social disablement which occurs with impaired work and social skills, and difficulties with personal relationships. These can be made worse by the response of other people, particularly when symptoms cause social comment or sanction.

——— Diagnosis

Over a period of weeks or months before the onset of schizophrenia the sufferer may lose interest in work, social activities, personal appearance and hygiene, and experience anxiety, depression and become preoccupied. This is called the prodromal phase.

The medical approach to diagnosis depends on the patient's symptoms falling into various categories. The International Classification of Diseases System (ICD-10, 1992) normally requires a minimum of one very clear symptom (and usually two or more if less clear cut) belonging to groups A to D (above), or symptoms from at least two of groups E to H should have been present for most of the time for at least one month.

Symptoms in group I in the list apply only to the diagnosis of simple schizophrenia and a duration of at least one year is required.

The diagnosis of schizophrenia should not be made in the presence of severe depression or manic symptoms unless the schizophrenic illness pre-dated a mood disturbance. If schizophrenic and mood symptoms develop together and are evenly balanced, a diagnosis of schizo-affective disorder is sometimes made. Also, schizophrenia should not be diagnosed where there is an obvious brain disease or during drug intoxication or withdrawal.

The main American diagnostic criteria (DSM-IV, 1994) for a diagnosis of schizophrenia are fairly precise and are shown below for comparison.

A. Characteristic symptoms

■ Two (or more) of the following, are noticeable for a significant portion of time during a one-month period (or less if successfully treated):

(1) Delusions
(2) Hallucinations
(3) Disorganized speech
(4) Grossly disorganized or catatonic behaviour
(5) Negative symptoms

B Social/occupational dysfunction

■ For a large portion of the time since the start of the disturbance, one or more major areas of life such as work, interpersonal relations, or self-care decline. When the onset is in childhood or adolescence, patients may not reach expected levels of interpersonal, educational or occupational achievement.

C Duration

■ Continuous signs of the disturbance persist for at least six months. This six-month period must include at least one month of symptoms (or less if successfully treated) that meet Criterion A and may include periods of prodromal or residual symptoms. During these prodromal or residual periods, the signs of the disturbance may be only negative symptoms, or else mild forms of two or more of the symptoms listed in Criterion A may be present. The diagnosis must rule out the possibility of the condition being due to the direct physiological effects of drugs (abuse or a medication), or a general medical condition.

Adapted form DSM–IV

——— Pattern of the illness

There are three basic patterns of schizophrenic illness:

1. Bouts of illness with acute symptoms, few negative symptoms, often with obvious causes, and followed by a good recovery.
2. Chronic illness with negative symptoms and disturbance of thinking processes, but few signs of acute illness, no obvious causes and with social isolation, withdrawal and odd behaviour. The outlook here is usually poor.
3. A combination of acute illness and gradually increasing chronic difficulties.

——— Types of schizophrenia

——— PARANOID SCHIZOPHRENIA

This is the commonest form of schizophrenic illness in which the patient usually suffers from stable delusions, usually accompanied by hearing voices (auditory hallucinations) and disturbances of perception. The onset tends to be later than in other forms of schizophrenia. The course of paranoid schizophrenia may be in bouts with partial or complete recovery, or chronic. When it is chronic, symptoms persist over years.

Paranoid delusions include:
Feelings of being persecuted, being referred to in the News, being of Royal birth, on a special mission to save mankind, having bodily changes, or of unaccountable jealousy.
Hallucinatory voices may threaten the patient or give commands; or sounds such as whistling, humming or laughing are heard
Hallucinations of smell or taste, or of sexual or other bodily sensations, and visual hallucinations sometimes occur.

——— HEBEPHRENIC SCHIZOPHRENIA

This form of schizophrenia usually starts with negative symptoms between the ages of 15 and 25 years and tends to have a poor prognosis. In this form of schizophrenia mood changes are to the fore, delusions and hallucinations are less striking, and behaviour tends to be irresponsible and unpredictable. The patient's mood tends to be shallow and inappropriate to the circumstances, often accompanied by giggling or self-satisfied smiling, or by a peculiar manner, with grimaces and pranks. Thought seems disorganised and speech is rambling and not sensible. There is a tendency for the patients to remain solitary.

CATATONIC SCHIZOPHRENIA

Disturbances of movement are the main abnormality and alternate between extremes of excitement and stupor and mutism, automatic obedience to instructions or apparently negative responses to instructions. Bodily postures may be maintained for long periods and episodes of violent excitement can occur. Catatonic schizophrenia is now rarely seen.

UNDIFFERENTIATED SCHIZOPHRENIA

Illnesses meeting the criteria for schizophrenia, but not conforming to any of the above sub-types, or showing features of more than one are called undifferentiated schizophrenia.

SIMPLE SCHIZOPHRENIA

Simple schizophrenia is a difficult diagnosis to make. It is an uncommon condition in which there is slowly worsening odd conduct, inability to cope, and decline in behaviour. The illness is less obviously schizophrenic than the other sub-types. Negative symptoms develop without being preceded by obvious acute symptoms. The individual may then become idle and aimless and vagrancy results.

RESIDUAL SCHIZOPHRENIA

This is a chronic stage in the development of a schizophrenic illness in which there has been clear progression from an early stage with acute symptoms to a later stage with long-term negative symptoms. Usually the patient is underactive in thought and behaviour, has a flat mood, is passive and lacks initiative, has little speech, and poor communication – flat facial expression, poor eye contact, self-care and social behaviour. There should be absence of dementia or other organic brain disease, and of chronic depression or institutionalization, sufficient to explain the negative symptoms.

POST-SCHIZOPHRENIC DEPRESSION

This is a depressive illness which may be prolonged, arising after a schizophrenic illness, some symptoms of which may still be present. Depressive symptoms are rarely sufficiently severe or extensive to meet criteria for a severe depressive episode, and it is difficult to decide which of the patient's symptoms are due to depression and which to medication, or to the negative symptoms of schizophrenia. This depression has an increased risk of suicide.

Schizo-affective disorders

These are episodic illnesses in which both mood and schizophrenic symptoms are present at the same time. Patients who suffer from recurrent schizo-affective illness, particularly those whose symptoms are of the manic rather than the depressive type, usually make a full recovery.

Some patients have recurrent schizo-affective illnesses which may be of the manic or depressive type or a mixture of the two. Others have one or two schizo-affective illnesses interspersed between typical bouts of mania or depression.

SCHIZO-AFFECTIVE DISORDER – MANIC TYPE

Schizophrenic and manic symptoms are present in the same episode of illness. The mood usually takes the form of elation, accompanied by increased self-esteem and grandiose ideas, but sometimes excitement or irritability are more obvious and accompanied by aggressive behaviour and persecutory ideas. There is increased energy, over-activity, impaired concentration, and a loss of normal social inhibition. Delusions of reference, grandeur or persecution may be present but other more typically schizophrenic symptoms are required to make the diagnosis. Manic type schizo-affective disorders, are usually florid with an acute onset. Behaviour is often grossly disturbed but with treatment full recovery generally occurs within a few weeks.

SCHIZO-AFFECTIVE DISORDER – DEPRESSIVE TYPE

Schizophrenic and depressive symptoms are present in the same episode of illness. Depressed mood is usually accompanied by symptoms such as slow thought, speech and movement, insomnia, loss of energy, appetite or weight, reduction of normal interests, impairment of concentration, guilt, feelings of hopelessness, and suicidal thoughts. Other more typically schizophrenic symptoms are present; patients may insist that their thoughts are being broadcast or interfered with, or that alien forces are trying to control them. They may be convinced that they are being spied upon or plotted against. Schizo-affective episodes of the depressive type are usually less dramatic than schizo-affective episodes of the manic type, but they tend to last longer and the outlook is less favourable. Although the majority of patients recover completely with treatment, some eventually have lasting impairment.

References

ICD-10 (1992): *Classification of Mental and Behavioural Disorders. Clinical descriptions and diagnostic guidelines.* World Health Organisation: Geneva.

DSM-IV (1994): *Diagnostic and Statistical Manual of Mental Disorders.* American Psychiatric Association: Washington DC.

2 What causes schizophrenia?

───── **Schizophrenia is a disease of the brain**

It used to be thought that schizophrenia was a 'functional' disorder, by which it was meant that there was no sign of brain disease or brain damage, unlike the 'organic' disorders such as Alzheimer's disease or head injuries. All sorts of psychological and social theories were put forward to explain why some people developed schizophrenia. Some psychoanalysts suggested that certain patterns of parenting and upbringing could confuse children so much that they developed schizophrenia in later life. There was really no scientific basis for such theories, which seemed to blame parents and caused them unnecessary self-doubts and guilty feelings. Not surprisingly, this did not help the relationship between the parents and the doctors, nor between the parents and their children with schizophrenia.

It is now well established, however, that abnormalities of the structure and function of the brain are present in the large majority of people suffering from schizophrenia. Post-mortem studies first suggested that the brains of people with schizophrenia were slightly smaller than usual and had abnormally large ventricles (the ventricles are the fluid-filled spaces in the middle of the brain). Over the last 15 years these changes have been confirmed by studies of brain scans (both computerised tomography (CT) scans and magnetic resonance imaging (MRI) scans).

■ **Abnormalities of the structure and function of the brain
are present in the large majority of people with schizophrenia**

These changes in the brain are subtle and amount to only around a 5% reduction in brain tissue. The changes are not so severe that the person's memory or level of intelligence are significantly affected, but they do seem to be the prime cause of the distressing symptoms and behaviour problems described in Chapter 1. Brain scans cannot be used to diagnose schizophrenia as the changes are only slight and easy to miss in any individual case. There is a big overlap between people with schizophrenia and the general population in terms of brain size.

Research is in progress into the causes of these changes in schizophrenia. It has been known for many years now that there is a genetic factor in the disorder. In other words schizophrenia tends to run in some families. However, this is not the whole story as factors in the environment seem to be important too.

────── Genetic factors

The chances of a person developing schizophrenia are increased if there is already someone in the family with the disorder. Risks are higher if a very close relative has schizophrenia, but not much higher than the general population's risk if it is present only in an uncle or aunt or a cousin.

Schizophrenia could be more common in certain families because relatives are more likely to share a similar upbringing. However, when the child of someone with schizophrenia is adopted by another family, the increased risk does not go away, which proves it is carried in their genes and cannot be explained simply as a result of being brought up in a particular way.

It is unlikely that a single abnormal gene is responsible for schizophrenia. Probably several genes are involved. Research on chromosomes is in progress which might discover these genes in the next few years. However, this is unlikely to lead to new ways of treating the disorder in the foreseeable future.

The genetic factor in schizophrenia

Affected relative	Risk of schizophrenia
Identical twin	46%
Non-identical twin	16%
Parent	14%
Sibling	9%
Grandparent	6%
Uncle or aunt	4%
Cousin	2%
No affected relative	**1%**

It is important to remember that, although the risk of schizophrenia in the child of a sufferer is increased to 14%, or one in seven, this still means that six out of seven children will *not* develop the disorder. Similarly, whilst a brother or sister (known as a 'sibling') of a sufferer has an increased risk of 9%, this still means that more than nine out of ten siblings will *not* develop schizophrenia. Overall, more than 60% of people with schizophrenia have no close family history of the disorder. What is inherited is not a certainty of developing the disorder but a tendency to do so, which then depends on other factors during a person's development.

Early brain development and schizophrenia

When the brains of people with schizophrenia have been studied under the microscope, the kinds of changes seen in the tissues suggest to the experts that the problems must start many years before schizophrenia develops in young adult life – most likely during the very early stages of brain development, either in the developing fetus (embryo) or around the time of birth. This has prompted researchers to look for possible causes of interference with brain development in people with schizophrenia, right back to the time they were in their mother's womb, and to circumstances surrounding their birth.

Virus infections and schizophrenia

It has been noted for some time that people with schizophrenia are more likely to have been born in the winter or early spring rather than in the summer or autumn months. This suggested to some researchers that virus infections, which are more frequent in the winter, might have affected schizophrenia sufferers whilst they were being carried in their mother's womb. In 1957 there was a severe epidemic of the virus infection influenza (flu). Researchers in Helsinki later found that schizophrenia was more common among the children of women who would have been six to nine months pregnant at the time of the flu epidemic. The increased risk was slight, and at most could explain only around one in twenty cases of the disorder. It seemed to be more of a factor among women sufferers of schizophrenia rather than men.

Birth difficulties

A number of studies have found that a past history of birth difficulties or obstetric complications is more common among people with schizophrenia. These include difficult deliveries, perhaps involving forceps or Caesarian sections, and breathing problems at birth or other complications which might have increased the risk of damage to the baby's brain. Again, such problems could explain only a small proportion of cases of schizophrenia. Birth complications seem to be more of a factor among men with schizophrenia rather than women.

Developmental problems during childhood

If damage to the brain in schizophrenia occurs in the womb or at the time of birth, it seems likely that people who eventually go on to develop the disorder might have problems during their childhood. There is some evidence that excessive anxiety and difficult behaviours are more likely among children who later go on to develop schizophrenia. Some researchers also believe that subtle disorders of movement and co-ordination may be present before the full illness develops. These problems, if indeed they are present, are not easy to spot. It is certainly not possible to tell from a child's movement or behaviour whether the child is at increased risk of developing schizophrenia as a teenager or young adult. The large majority of children with anxiety or difficult behaviour will *not* develop schizophrenia, even if they have a relative with the disorder.

The neurodevelopmental hypothesis

The theory outlined above, involving damage to the brain very early in development, many years before the onset of severe symptoms, is known as the *neurodevelopmental hypothesis*. It may explain other observations about schizophrenia, including the fact that it is more likely in a person whose mother suffered from malnutrition during pregnancy. Schizophrenia is also more common among young people born and brought up in the middle of cities. This may be due to the increased risk of catching a virus infection in more overcrowded living conditions.

All the research that has been done so far is consistent in one respect: *there is no evidence that schizophrenia can be blamed on a person's parents or upbringing.* There is no way at present of predicting which children might go on to develop schizophrenia, and therefore no way of preventing an increased risk in some young people.

Possible environmental causes of schizophrenia

- Virus infection of the developing baby in the womb
- Malnutrition of the mother during pregnancy
- Birth difficulties and complications
- Being born and raised in the inner city

Whatever the *underlying causes* of the increased tendency to develop schizophrenia in a particular young person, the disorder often starts after some *precipitating cause* in the person's life.

Precipitating causes

Studies of the events around the time of the initial development of schizophrenia have shown that the illness often starts after a stressful time or an unhappy event in the person's life. This might be the loss of a job, a bereavement in the family, the break-up of a relationship, or worries about finances or accommodation. An early sign of schizophrenia may be worry about such problems which seems out of all proportion to those closest to the sufferer. This can be apparent for some time before more serious symptoms develop, such as hallucinations or delusions (see Chapter 1). These life events and difficulties *in themselves* would not be sufficient to cause serious psychiatric illness unless the person already had an underlying vulnerability and predisposition to develop schizophrenia, which has arisen due to the causes listed above.

────── Drug and alcohol misuse

Sometimes the onset of schizophrenia seems to be related to drinking too much alcohol. Again, drinking too much does not *cause* schizophrenia by itself. It is simply a precipitating factor which leads to significant illness only where the underlying tendency to develop schizophrenia is already present.

Misuse of some drugs has been found to lead to illnesses which are very similar to schizophrenia, with symptoms such as delusions, hallucinations, and disturbance of behaviour. In particular, this type of problem can result from the use of stimulants such as *amphetamines* ('speed', 'whizz', 'uppers', 'sulphate'), and *cocaine* ('coke', 'snow', 'crack', 'freebase', 'base'). These illnesses, known as *drug-induced psychoses*, are usually short-lived, perhaps lasting only a few days or weeks at the most. However, if the person has an underlying predisposition or vulnerability to develop schizophrenia then they may not recover so quickly but instead may go on to develop the full illness and its longer term problems.

Precipitating causes of schizophrenia

- Adverse life events
     losing a job, bereavement,
     the break-up of a relationship, etc.
- Alcohol misuse
     (more than two small drinks per day)
- Drugs
     stimulants (amphetamines, cocaine)
     hallucinogenics (LSD, magic mushrooms, angel dust)

Other drugs can cause hallucinations when taken, but the effects wear off almost immediately and the drugs do not cause a psychotic illness. These hallucinogenic drugs include *lysergic acid diethylamide* ('LSD' or 'acid'), *magic mushrooms* ('Liberty

Cap' or 'Fly agaric'), and *phencyclidine* ('PCP' or 'angel dust').

Anyone who has suffered from schizophrenia should ideally avoid drinking too much alcohol (perhaps stick to one or two drinks per day, and then only at the weekend) and should definitely avoid taking any stimulant or hallucinogenic drugs, to reduce the risk of having a relapse of their illness.

―――― Avoiding stress

Since stressful life events seem to precipitate schizophrenia, it is important that people who have recovered from a previous episode of schizophrenia should try and reduce sources of stress in their lives in order to try and avoid a relapse of their condition.

Sometimes it seems to the people close to the sufferer that it would be good for them to get back to work or college and to resume all the things in their life which had to stop whilst they were ill. However, going back to work, particularly if it is a stressful job, may lead to anxiety which could increase the risk of relapse. It may be too much to expect, especially straight after an episode of schizophrenia, that the sufferer can pick up where they left off, play a full part in life again, and fulfil the expectations of family, girlfriend or boyfriend, or employer. Some people who have suffered from schizophrenia seem to want to spend much more time by themselves, perhaps being alone in their rooms for hours on end. If they are forced to interact more with other people they may find it so stressful that they develop more symptoms and suffer a relapse.

On the other hand, if people with schizophrenia are not usefully employed in some activity on most days, then they can become more withdrawn, very quiet, almost emotionless, and apathetic, not bothering much about looking after themselves and their belongings (these are the *negative* symptoms of schizophrenia, see Chapter 1).

This means a balance has to be struck between *over-stimulation*, involving many activities, contacts with others, and expectations of the person to work and socialise on the one hand, and *under-stimulation*, leaving the person to spend all day alone in their room, on the other.

Families or other carers struggling to find this correct balance should be able to obtain help and advice from the psychiatrist, mental health nurse (community psychiatric nurse or CPN) or occupational therapist (OT) who are members of the community mental health team. One area these professionals are quite likely to want to discuss with the family or other carers is the way that they should talk to the person with schizophrenia, especially in terms of expressing any emotions and feelings they might have towards them.

──── Expressed emotion

Expressed emotion includes *critical remarks* and *hostility* towards the sufferer, but also expressions of *emotional over-involvement*, with over-protectiveness, and high expectations of close contact and demonstrations of affection that the sufferer may be unable to give.

Studies going back to the 1960s have shown that high levels of *expressed emotion* by the carers can increase the risk of a relapse for the person with schizophrenia. Where there is a high level of expressed emotion the risk of relapse may be doubled in the first year after recovery from an episode of the illness. Therefore avoiding high expressed emotion is as important as continuing to take medication in terms of avoiding a relapse.

It is not surprising that the family or other carers may develop a whole range of emotional responses to the person with schizophrenia. The person's behaviour may be socially disruptive, embarrassing, or frustrating. Carers may feel anger at such behaviour, guilt because the person is ill, grief at losing the person the sufferer used to be before the illness struck, worries about how they will manage in the future, and isolation from contact with the rest of the world. The negative symptoms in particular are not easy to understand and forgive, and may be seen as laziness, which is not usually the case. However, expressing such emotions to the sufferer will often increase their anxiety and make a relapse of their schizophrenia more likely. The carers may need some considerable time and professional help to learn how best to deal with the sufferer.

Carers need to find the right balance between allowing the person with schizophrenia the time and space they need to be alone, whilst encouraging a reasonable level of day to day activity and contact with life. What has been shown to be helpful to the sufferer are expressions of warmth and support, which may sometimes have to be given without any great expectations of such expressions in return.

How to live with someone with schizophrenia

- Give them space and time alone if they need it
- Encourage some activity and socialising every day
- Try to avoid criticising them (not at all easy sometimes)
- Try to avoid overprotection or smothering with kindness
- Try to accept the sufferer may not be able to express their love or gratitude in return
- Try to offer the sufferer warmth and support
- Seek professional advice if tensions are running high

Avoiding high levels of expressed emotion and finding the right balance between over- and under-stimulation are often not easy things to accomplish. Help should be available in terms of professional advice and support, and sometimes **respite care**. These issues are dealt with in later chapters.

3 Medical treatment

Effective early treatment improves the long-term outlook for people with schizophrenia. Most first episodes of schizophrenia occur in adolescence or early adult life, and the correct initial treatment is crucial. Symptoms of schizophrenia can be controlled by medication. However, the distressing and severe side-effects of older drugs causes some people to stop taking their drugs (*non-compliance*). Abandoning drug therapy almost always causes relapses, and can result in admission to hospital. The newer antipsychotic drugs are as effective in treating symptoms and have fewer side-effects. Patients can be encouraged to stick to their medication if their family is supported and taught about the value of treatment.

Schizophrenia accounts for nearly 10% of the total NHS inpatient budget, more than any other illness. With the emphasis on care in the community there is a need for better use of a wide range of treatments – from medication to talking treatments and other therapies; effective early intervention and better information and help for patients, carers and relatives. The more patients with schizophrenia who are managed in the community, the more team work is needed between general practitioners, psychiatrists and community mental health teams.

──── Drug treatment

■ Drug treatment, together with social and psychological approaches, is an essential part of treatment.

Drug treatment is best used to control acute psychotic symptoms and to prevent relapse in the longer term.

Drugs used in the treatment of schizophrenia are called antipsychotic, or neuroleptic, drugs. Older drugs include: chlorpromazine, thioridazine, fluphenazine, haloperidol, flupenthixol and pimozide. They are classified according to their different chemical structures, and all appear to work by blocking a chemical messenger, dopamine, at nerve endings in the brain. Antipsychotic drugs are intended to calm the patient without making them drowsy or causing excitement.

These drugs can relieve symptoms in most patients, but in some improvement is only partial. There tends to be more improvement in symptoms such as delusions and hallucinations (positive symptoms) than symptoms such as social withdrawal and apathy (negative symptoms). All drugs can produce unwanted effects such as trembling, stillness, abnormal face and body movements, restlessness, and tardive dyskinesia (involuntary movements, usually facial, which generally occur after years of medication). Many of these unwanted effects disappear if treatment is withdrawn or reduced or medication is given to counteract them. However, giving drugs routinely to stop side-effects is not justified , since not all patients are affected and because in some cases side effects may be worsened.

Acute treatment

> ■ Drug treatment with antipsychotic medication should be started as soon as possible once an accurate diagnosis is made.

Any delay could mean a poorer long-term outcome. The patient's overall behaviour is likely to improve quickly, but some acute symptoms of illness may take weeks or months to go away completely. It is not possible to match an antipsychotic drug to a particular patient. Some drugs (eg. chlorpromazine) are more sedative than others and this may be a benefit or a drawback depending on the circumstances.

Medication takes several weeks to reach its full effect. If some troublesome symptoms persist after six weeks, drug treatment may be increased for a further short period or a different class of antipsychotic drug may be tried instead. Benzodiazepine tranquillizers may help control symptoms in very disturbed and aggressive patients, which may allow lower doses of antipsychotic medication to be used and hence fewer side-effects. In an emergency, medication may need to be given by injection to restrain a violent patient.

Around one in ten patients will remain permanently well after stopping drug treatment following a first schizophrenic illness – but they are hard to predict. Nor is it possible to identify patients in whom continued (maintenance) treatment is not needed after acute illness, or patients whose maintenance therapy can be stopped without risk of relapse.

——— **Maintenance treatment**

> ■ Because of the risk of relapse it is usually advised that medication is taken for years, sometimes for life.

Continued (maintenance) treatment with antipsychotic medication reduces that risk. After an acute illness, patients relapse at a rate of about one in ten for each month without medication, even if treatment is withdrawn after years of successful maintenance treatment. In patients who continue their medication the relapse rate is halved. Continuous drug treatment is better than taking time off medication.

Factors that are important in deciding whether or not to continue or withdraw maintenance medication include risks to the patient if they relapse, their ability to tolerate medication, the level of social support available, and the views of the patient, relatives and carers.

Maintenance treatment may be given orally or by 'depot' injection, usually every two to four weeks but sometimes less or more frequently. Depot injections are absorbed slowly and provide therapeutic levels of the drug between injections. The use of depot injections at 'depot clinics' also gives the opportunity for regular review, monitoring and patient contact. Injections usually remove the need to take tablets every day but they may be painful and so changing the site of injection at each visit is sensible. Depot treatment should be supplemented with oral treatment if the patient is under stress or shows signs of relapse as the depot will probably not work quickly enough in this situation. Depot treatment is best for patients treated in the community, since they may not take their oral treatment and this may result in readmission to hospital.

▬▬▬ Unwanted side effects

■ These are common, but are usually a nuisance rather than a serious problem.

Extrapyramidal effects
(stiffness and trembling, like Parkinson's disease)
This occurs in about a third of patients and can be treated with anti-parkinsonian drugs, (eg., benzhexol, benztropine, orphenadrine, and procyclidine).

Acute dystonic reactions
(sudden onset of stiffness and rigidity, sometimes with eye-rolling, that is painful and distressing)
This can be rapidly treated with anti-parkinsonian drugs.

Akathisia
(this is a distressing sensation of inner and motor restlessness which can be mistaken for the agitation of acute illness)

Tardive dyskinesia
(lasting uncontrollable movements, initially affecting the face, lips and tongue)

This affects up to 20% of patients over the long-term, 10% of whom are severely affected. The risk is higher in older patients. Antipsychotic drugs should be used at the lowest possible dose to limit the occurrence of tardive dyskinesia.

Muscarinic effects
(dry mouth, blurred vision, constipation, difficulty passing water, confusion and fast heart rate).

Anti-alpha adrenergic effects
(dizziness when standing up quickly)

Antihistaminic effects
(drowsiness – often troublesome, especially in older people)

———— NEUROLEPTIC MALIGNANT SYNDROME

A dramatic, rare, at times fatal, reaction seen most commonly early in treatment. Typical features are muscular rigidity, low body temperature, fluctuating consciousness and unstable blood pressure, and heart rate. Treatment in a hospital intensive care unit is needed initially.

———— OTHER EFFECTS

These include weight gain, convulsions, jaundice, lowering of white blood cell counts, skin sensitivity to sunlight, contact dermatitis and rashes, and chlorpromazine and thioridazine may cause pigmentation of the skin, cornea or lens. Sexual dysfunction can affect both men and women. Antipsychotic drugs cross the placenta in pregnant women and are present in breast milk. If antipsychotic medication is needed in these situations it should be given in the lowest possible dose.

There have been rare reports of sudden death occurring in people on antipsychotic medication, but a direct link is not proven. The risk is not fully understood. All medicines have potentially serious effects and it is always a case of balancing the risks and benefits: the benefits of antipsychotic drugs far outweigh the ill effects.

Abrupt withdrawal of antipsychotic drugs occasionally produces symptoms such as feelings of sickness, abdominal pain, diarrhoea, restlessness, sleep problems and may worsen involuntary movements. Therefore, the dose should be reduced gradually.

———— Interactions with other drugs

Alcohol and sedative medication increase drowsiness in people taking antipsychotic treatment. The older established antidepressant drugs increase the blood level of antipsychotic drugs and patients may be at risk of heart irregularities. Antipsychotic drugs can also complicate treatment with anti-epilepsy drugs and may lead to seizures. Antipsychotic drugs taken with lithium, a mood-stabilising drug, may lead to excitation, restlessness, muscle rigidity and raised temperature.

Compliance

> ■ Poor compliance with treatment is common and is an important cause of relapse.

This occurs in one-third of inpatients and two-thirds of patients in the community. Patients may abandon their treatments because of inadequate information, difficulty in managing the treatment doses, denial of illness, and forgetfulness. Some patients do not feel well on, or see the benefits of, medication, even though their symptoms have improved and so they are tempted to stop medication. Unwanted effects of medication, especially trembling, stiffness and involuntary movements, often lead patients not to take their medication. Patients and carers need to know the nature and purpose of the treatment, including any possible unwanted effects. GPs and psychiatrists are able to provide this information.

It is important to ensure that patients do not lapse from treatment and therefore the simplest treatment regimen should be used. The patient should be observed for, and questioned specifically about, unwanted effects which may be lessened by reducing the dose or by changing medication to a better tolerated drug.

Depression

Over half of patients have depressive symptoms during an acute illness, and this occurs in a quarter to a half during the recovery phase. Depression may be difficult to tell from the negative symptoms of schizophrenia, and from some drug-induced side-effects that make the patient look depressed. Antidepressant medication is effective for the treatment of depression in people with schizophrenia.

Treatment resistance

Some patients seem resistant to treatment – defined as failure to achieve satisfactory relief of symptoms despite a good trial of three different types of antipsychotic drug, each given in proper doses for at least six weeks. Factors in the patient's social situation that might aggravate acute symptoms should be considered, including high levels of stress or the use of illicit drugs. Blood levels of antipsychotic drugs can be measured to identify patients who are not taking their medication as prescribed, or who require a higher or lower dose. Higher doses of medication, however, do not solve the problem of treatment resistance.

Changing to a different drug can help to overcome treatment resistance. Lithium, a mood stabilizer, and lorazepam, a tranquillizer, appear to improve the effectiveness of antipsychotic drugs, particularly where there are symptoms of mood disorder or anxiety. Carbamazepine, another mood stabilizer, and propranolol, for anxiety symptoms, have also been used in this situation.

Positive and negative symptoms, behaviour and social function improve with clozapine, but excess salivation, drowsiness, weight gain, and fast heart rate are
unwanted effects, and convulsions may occur. However, involuntary movements
are rare, and established tardive dyskinesia may improve. The most serious
unwanted effect of clozapine is a lowering of the blood white cell count (agranulo-
cytosis), which puts patients at risk of serious infection. This occurs approximately
ten times more frequently with clozapine than with older established antipsychotic
drugs and the drug is restricted to patients who are registered with the Clozaril
Patient Monitoring Service, which ensures regular monitoring of white blood cell
counts. Treatment is stopped if the white cell count falls below a standard level.

——— Newer drugs

Newer drugs tend to act on different chemical messengers than the older drugs
and so are less likely to cause side-effects and can help negative symptoms. Some
of the newer, atypical, drugs require blood pressure monitoring during the early
stages of treatment.

Drugs used in psychoses and related disorders (tablets and syrup)

Chlorpromazine	Perphenazine
Benperidol	Pimozide
Clozapine	Prochlorperazine
Droperidol	Promazine
Flupenthixol	Risperidone
Fluphenazine	Sertindole
Haloperidol	Sulpiride
Loxapine	Thioridazine
Methotrimeprazine	Trifluoperazine
Olanzapine	Zuclopenthixol
Oxypertine	Zuclopenthixol Dihydrochloride
Pericyazine	

Antipsychotic depot preparations (injections)
Flupenthixol Decanoate
Fluphenazine Decanoate
Haloperidol Decanoate
Pipothiazine Palmitate
Zuclopenthixol Decanoate

4 The family, the community and talking treatments

Medication treats acute and some negative symptoms of schizophrenia but does not always give a complete cure. The support of family and friends, community care, talking treatments and rehabilitation are all essential too. A 'care package' consisting of all the elements that help an individual is what should be aimed for.

——— Family and friends

Family and friends are not the cause of schizophrenia. When someone you love has schizophrenia many questions and powerful emotions come out – blame, guilt, anger, worry, desperation, disbelief – and there is a sense of isolation and being stigmatised.

> ■ Family and friends need support, information and advice but are frequently left to shoulder the burden alone, and often feel that no-one understands or cares.

The general practitioner, members of the local mental health team and voluntary groups are far more able to give support than in the past and are ready to respond to individuals concerns and crises.

The task of helping a loved-one (which often falls to mothers and wives) can continue over years and can be draining – as well as rewarding. Family relationships and friendships change because of the effect schizophrenia has on communication, closeness and behaviour. Carers may unexpectedly have to become the sole provider for the family, with all that that entails, and still have to encourage the sufferer in all manner of day-to-day activities – making friends, taking up interests and hobbies, washing, shopping and using the telephone.

——— Coping

> ■ Carers need to learn as much as they can about schizophrenia, its treatment, and how to recognise warning signs and who to turn to for help when it is needed.

Caring for someone with schizophrenia sometimes means learning the hard way. Experience will show that some ideas work, and others don't. The simple advice is to keep trying things that work and avoid those that don't.

Getting frustrated with a person with schizophrenia probably won't work and may even make things worse. Problems need to be tackled calmly and one at a time. Pushing too hard can create stress that may worsen symptoms. It is a difficult balance. Taking over too much, becoming over involved, is usually right at times of acute illness but at other times 'doing too much' can be counter-productive and hinder the person trying out their skills and gaining much needed confidence, even with simple tasks and chores.

Stress

■ If there is too much stress at home and everyone is suffering a solution that may have to be considered is living apart while keeping in regular contact.

People with schizophrenia are usually badly affected by family stress. Types of stress that are harmful are when there are many critical comments about the person; hostility or anger towards the person; and when relatives become too involved emotionally with the person.

Family-based talking treatment which teaches people how to avoid these traps cuts down the number of relapses but is not available everywhere – you may have to ask.

Too much stimulation of this sort is to be avoided, but so is not enough stimulation – this can lead the patient to become more withdrawn and isolated.

Community care

This is a term to love or hate – sometimes it seems to produce the results that really help sufferers and carers and at other times it seems to fail. What community care should do is to provide full local support for people with mental illness.

What people should expect locally

- Involvement in choosing what care or treatment is offered
- Integration into the community and its activities
- Protection from abuse
- Periods of asylum – peace and rest – when necessary
- Relief from distress
- To be noticed when in need
- Help with finances, housing, leisure and employment
- Help at any time around the clock
- Help for life, including with medical and psychiatric treatment
- Protection as regards legal matters

After leaving hospital the first person to turn to is usually the family doctor, who tends to be involved in day-to-day medical problems and at times of crisis. Usually there will also be a key worker (often a community psychiatric nurse) who should coordinate care and be a link between the sufferer, the family, the general practitioner and the mental health team.

Apart from medical and psychiatric treatment the main types of help are:

- Discussing problems caused by disturbed behaviour and coming up with ways of improving behaviour or coping with it.
- Discussing feelings and reactions to illness – it can be helpful to share concerns and ideas and correct misunderstandings and to have as realistic an understanding of the person, their illness and the future as possible.
- Reducing feelings of isolation and stigma by meeting people who really do understand – others in the same situation, for example in self-help and voluntary groups – who can share experiences, the latest information, and provide support as well as understanding.
- The churches, religious organisations and the police are usually very ready to help too.

Looking after yourself

There are plenty of reasons to be hopeful even when things seem desperate. People with schizophrenia can get better after long illnesses and new drugs and talking treatments are being introduced all the time. Avoiding stress and keeping up interests and relaxation are powerful protections and give extra strength. Everyone needs to go at their own pace – not trying to do everything at once, but rather one step at a time, and taking each day as it comes.

Talking treatments

There is great interest in talking treatments. Several new types are being tried out at present to see how much good they do. One of the problems is that some patients do not think they are ill and, of course, this makes all treatments difficult, though talking treatments can still be used by family and carers.

Most work with patients and families aims to:

- Improve social and mental functioning
- Reduce the risk of relapse into illness
- Reduce the severity of symptoms
- Teach how to recognise and keep a check on warning signs and how to get help quickly
- Increase compliance with medication and treatment

Providing information, advice and practical support to patients and families is the main kind of talking treatment. When a person has acute symptoms, accepting that for that person the symptoms are real and distressing is vital, not blunt advice that their symptoms are imaginary. Showing the sufferer that symptoms, like delusions, are understood – though not shared – helps to built trust.

Ways in which carers can help the patient:

- Learning about the illness and its treatment, side effects, community care, and what is likely to happen in future
- Reducing stress in the family by recognising what causes stresses and avoiding them
- Increasing independence at a comfortable pace
- Tackling day-to-day problems by trying out practical solutions one at a time and seeing the effect
- Usually talking treatments occur in several sessions, over a period of months, with booster sessions after that, either at home or at the

> outpatient clinic or resource centre
> ■ Family work is not available everywhere, but increasingly community psychiatric nurses are being trained to make them available in most areas

Cognitive behavioural methods

These are aimed at changing ways of thinking and behaving. They can help lessen acute symptoms and distress by

■ encouraging healthy behaviour and talk

■ distracting attention from acute symptoms (like hearing voices)

■ altering beliefs caused by the illness (like delusions)

■ helping reduce stress in a number of ways, including relaxation.

Research is taking place to see if such talking treatments can be successful alone or are better in combination with medication.

Rehabilitation

People with schizophrenia who have been in hospital, often take differing amounts of time to adjust to new living situations and for some, independence seems, for the moment, unrealistic. Different individuals have different needs.

Accommodation

The range of accommodation to suit varying circumstances is wide:

■ Hostel wards
■ Hospital houses
■ Hostels with varying degrees of supervision
■ Staffed and unstaffed grouped homes
■ Supported lodgings
■ Independent flats

──── Care and therapy

Care and therapy can be given:

- At home
- Day hospital
- Day centre
- Drop-in centres
- Outpatient clinics
- Resource centres
- At the GP's surgery

──── Activity

People with schizophrenia should be able to progress at their own pace, starting simply with exercise or individual activity, and as the patient gains confidence and improves, moving back to a normal working life.

Activities

- Physical activities, for example keep-fit
- Recreation
- Occupational therapy
- Sheltered workshops; and, eventually,
- Paid employment

Most people with schizophrenia want to work and do work when they are not ill.

──── Other methods

There are many other types of therapy from psychoanalysis to primal scream therapy, and most of these are probably not particularly helpful for most people with schizophrenia, and some may do more harm than good. The same is probably true of complementary therapies, such as acupuncture, aromatherapy and herbal remedies. It is best always to talk to your doctor or key worker before starting on something which may cost a lot of money and do no good.

5 Access to care

The GP is the first port of call

Everyone in the United Kingdom has the right to be registered with a General Practitioner (GP), except for people who have been in hospital for longer than a year. People who move around from place to place may register with an NHS GP wherever they are staying, for three months at a time, as a 'temporary resident'.

■ It is best to take mental health problems to a GP first, rather than go straight to a hospital casualty department or psychiatric ward.

The GP will usually provide some treatment straight away, or refer the patient on to a specialist, or both. The GP will know the right person to refer a patient to. A casualty doctor may simply send a person away again if the mental health problem is not thought to be immediately urgent.

Home visits

The GP will visit the patient at home if necessary – for example if the person won't come to the surgery because they don't agree that they need help.

It is more time-consuming for the GP to make a home visit (four people can be seen in surgery in the same time it takes to visit one patient), and the equipment and facilities of the surgery are not available to the doctor in the patient's home. For these reasons it is better, if possible, that the patient makes an appointment to see the doctor.

On the other hand, if a patient with mental health problems won't go, because they don't recognise that they need help, or if they are not thinking clearly, or they have a problem concentrating, and so can't remember to turn up for their appointments, then the doctor should be asked to make a home visit. The doctor cannot refuse to visit a registered patient in need of such help as long

as the patient is staying at an address within the doctor's practice area (usually the same town as the doctor's surgery).

People who are not registered with a GP

If a person who is not already registered with a local doctor needs treatment in an emergency, then any GP must see that person as soon as possible, as long as the person is staying at an address within the GP's practice area. You may have to insist that the GP sees the person, and this only applies to real emergencies, where someone is seriously ill or at immediate risk of harming themselves or others.

It is important for all people with schizophrenia to be registered with a GP, especially those about to leave hospital, who should see the GP within a few days or so after discharge. The GP will usually provide repeat prescriptions of medication recommended by the specialist, as well as sickness certificates (sick notes) if necessary, and will also deal with the patient's physical health problems.

Getting the best out of your doctor

These days, all GPs should provide written details to patients of surgery times, how to go about making an appointment, how to ask for a repeat prescription, details of times when the GP is available to speak on the telephone, and how to request a home visit, either during the day, or 'out-of-hours' (in the evening or at the weekend). The GP's practice must also give details of how complaints and suggestions are handled. Ask your doctor's receptionist for their practice leaflet or booklet.

You will get the best out of your doctor by cooperating as much as possible with the surgery's arrangements for appointments, telephone calls, and visits. The doctor will appreciate it if you arrive on time for your appointment. If you can, please request a home visit before 10 o'clock in the morning, so the GP can plan his or her day more easily. Remember the GP has to see around forty or so patients every day, and sometimes is under quite a lot of pressure of time. The doctor may be even more helpful than usual if he or she feels that you have been helpful too.

It is best, if you can, to keep the number of problems you want to talk about down to two or three at the most for each appointment, as appointments usually last only about ten minutes. The GP will of course see you for longer if you have a particularly difficult problem that needs more time, but each appointment that goes on for fifteen or twenty minutes makes the doctor later for the other patients who are waiting.

You can always make another appointment to deal with any problems not covered in the first consultation, (as long as these problems can wait, of course). The other thing you might be able to do is to ask for a double appointment so that there is more time to discuss any problems, worries, or complaints that you have.

Don't be afraid to write down a list of things you want to say, or questions you want to ask, when you see the GP. Some doctors don't seem to like lists, but they will usually go through each point and answer each question carefully when asked. Don't be afraid also to take along a friend if you feel nervous or you are worried you won't be able to remember everything you need to say.

People whose first language is not English may need to take an interpreter along with them when they go to see the GP. General practices in areas where people of ethnic minorities are living in greater numbers may provide interpreters on request. The practice will usually provide written information on any arrangements in place for people of ethnic minorities.

If you are unhappy with something the GP does or does not do for you, or for your relative or friend with schizophrenia, it is best if you can to have a quiet word with the doctor first, rather than making an official complaint (see the section on how to complain below). Many disagreements can be quickly sorted out by speaking to the doctor or to the practice manager.

Getting the best out of your GP

- Ask for the practice leaflet or booklet
- Cooperate with the arrangements for requesting appointments and visits as much as possible
- If you can, stick to one or two problems only at each consultation
- Make a list of your problems or questions to help you remember
- Take along a friend or relative if you are nervous
- Ask for an interpreter if you need one
- Have a word with the doctor or practice manager first if you have any problems, before making an official complaint

Changing your GP

If you and your doctor simply cannot agree, or you cannot get on with your doctor, then you may change GPs by taking your NHS medical card along to another doctor's practice and asking to sign on there. If all the other local practices are full and say that they can't take you on their list, then you must telephone the Family Health Service Authority (FHSA) (now called the Primary Care Authority), whose number is on your NHS medical card, and also in the telephone book. The FHSA will find you a new GP within a few days at the most.

GPs have the right to refuse to continue to treat someone whom they feel they can't get on with. For example, if a patient is abusive, aggressive, or violent with the doctor or with the doctor's staff, then the patient can be removed from the doctor's list straight away. However, if that patient is suffering from mental health problems, then the GP must address those mental health problems before the patient can be removed from the doctor's list. This means either giving treatment or referring the person to the mental health services so that they can get help.

Mental health service teams

Mental health professionals usually work in teams including psychiatrists, mental health nurses, social workers, occupational therapists, and psychologists. The team will usually be called the *multidisciplinary community mental health team* or '*CMHT*'. These different professionals have different qualifications and play different roles within the team.

Psychiatrists

Psychiatrists are doctors who have completed six years in medical school learning about physical health care as well as mental health problems. They then spend several more years as specialists learning to look after mental health problems, working as 'senior house officers', 'registrars', or 'hospital practitioners', in mental hospital wards, psychiatric outpatient clinics, and outside hospitals with community mental health teams. To be 'consultant' psychiatrists, which is the most senior position, they must have passed the examination for the Membership of the Royal College of Psychiatrists and so have the letters MRCPsych after their names.

The psychiatrist's role in the team is to make a diagnosis and decide on treatment, which will often include medication such as tablets or injections. The psychiatrist is always involved when patients need admitting to hospital, whether voluntarily or under a Section of the Mental Health Act (see Chapter 6).

The psychiatrist, like all the mental health professionals in the team, will also spend time listening to patients' problems and offering advice and support. The psychiatrist is usually, though not always, the leader of the mental health team.

——— Mental health nurses

The mental health nurse, or community psychiatric nurse (CPN) is the professional who will usually give the patient any injections which have been prescribed by the psychiatrist. (Sometimes injections are given by the general practice nurse or by the GP.) However, the CPN is trained in many more aspects of mental health care than just giving medication.

The CPN will often work as a patient's *keyworker*, which means the professional who is the first point of contact for the patient or their carers, who stays in regular contact, and is responsible for making sure that the care planned for a patient is actually delivered. The CPN can also refer the patient to social services if they have social problems such as worries over money (including benefits), childcare, or housing.

The CPN is trained in assessing a person's mental state and deciding whether the person might need to see the psychiatrist for a review of their medication or other treatment. The CPN will also spend time listening to the patient's problems and offering support, advice, and counselling. The CPN may be trained in specific treatment techniques such as relaxation therapy and the management of anxiety symptoms.

The CPN is also trained in ways of educating patients, and their relatives or other carers, about illnesses such as schizophrenia which can be quite difficult to understand without careful explanation. The CPN can advise carers about what to do when they run into difficulties with their relatives with schizophrenia.

——— Social workers

Social workers are usually employed by the Local Authority (the Council), and are based in Social Services departments, unlike the other members of the CMHT who are employed by NHS hospitals or community trusts. However, in well-run community teams, the different members meet frequently and work closely together, despite the fact that they have different employers. The social worker may also be a person's keyworker.

The social worker is the expert on help with social problems, including money worries, how to claim social security benefits, housing – including council housing and residential group homes, respite care, child care such as childminding, and travel problems such as how to obtain bus passes.

Social workers may also be approved under the Mental Health Act to take part in assessing whether a patient should be admitted and detained compulsorily under a Section (see Chapter 6).

Occupational therapists

The special expertise of the occupational therapist, or OT, is helping patients develop their activities of daily living, which includes looking after themselves and their home, finding work outside the home which suits them, perhaps finding places for patients on educational or training courses to improve their work skills, or arranging other daytime activities which are helpful in a person's care.

The OT may also act as a patient's keyworker, and may also offer sympathetic listening, advice and counselling, and anxiety management, but is not trained to give medication.

Clinical psychologists

Unlike psychiatrists, clinical psychologists are not medically trained and therefore cannot prescribe or advise on medication. However, they also undergo a prolonged training, including a university degree in psychology, which equips them to offer specific psychological treatments.

These treatments include *cognitive therapy* which can be most helpful for patients with depression, *anxiety management* including relaxation exercises and treatments for phobias, and sometimes *group or family therapy* to help patients to improve their relationships with other people including their family or other carers. Some psychologists run groups for families and other carers of patients with schizophrenia, which provide an opportunity to discuss worries with others who know what it is like to look after a person with schizophrenia. Unfortunately, there are not very many of these groups provided by the NHS at the moment.

Clinical psychologists are less frequently involved in the care of people with schizophrenia than the other members of the CMHT, but they may also sometimes act as keyworkers for patients.

Crisis response teams

In some parts of the country, there is another mental health team in the community, known as the *Crisis Response Service* or *Mental Health Rapid Response Team*. This is a team of psychiatrists, CPNs, and social workers, which is on-call out-of-hours to deal with emergencies, when patients' problems suddenly become worse outside of normal office hours. The idea is that the teams can give patients rapid treatment and support within their own homes and so avoid the need for hospital admission.

Sometimes this team will be made up of the same people who work as the daytime community mental health team, but often it will be a separately staffed team which will deal with emergencies and then pass the patient back to the area CMHT in the morning.

Counsellors

In recent years, there has been a big increase in the numbers of counsellors employed by GPs to help their patients with emotional problems. Counsellors vary in their experience and qualifications, but should usually be accredited or approved by the British Association of Counselling (BAC).

Counselling means listening. Counsellors listen to a person with emotional problems, reflect back to the person what they feel are the main priorities to deal with, and so help the person to start to tackle their problems themselves.

Counsellors may sometimes be involved with the care of a person with schizophrenia. However, their special expertise lies in listening and helping the person to help themselves. Such an approach is not usually effective when people with schizophrenia are seriously ill and suffering from hallucinations and delusions, because to help themselves people need insight into their own problems, and in schizophrenia people often do not recognise that they need help.

Counsellors are not usually trained as doctors or nurses and so do not usually advise on medication. They should be in regular contact with their client's GP, but do not usually meet other members of the CMHT. People with a complex problem like schizophrenia should usually be looked after by the community mental health team, which can offer the various different kinds of help from the different professionals listed above.

The Care Programme Approach

In the old days, all the services and facilities involved in the care of someone with a serious mental health problem like schizophrenia were under one roof, in the large mental hospital. Now that most people with such problems live outside hospital there is a risk that they won't get all the care which they need. That is because the services in the community are all managed separately, including health services, social services, social security, and housing.

To make sure that the different community services are coordinated and all work together in a particular person's care, the Care Programme Approach, or CPA, was introduced in 1991. The CPA requires professionals from the health authority and the local authority to get together to arrange care.

The CPA applies to all patients accepted for care by the specialist mental health services. It requires first of all that a professional meets with the patient and carries out an *assessment of need.* Then a care plan should be drawn up (and written down) which addresses a person's needs, social as well as medical and nursing needs. A meeting may be held between the different professionals involved to plan a person's care. The person with schizophrenia will be invited to attend this meeting, along with their family or other carers if the person agrees that they may also attend. Such a *care-planning meeting* commonly takes place before a person is discharged from hospital.

To make sure the plan is followed, one professional, often a CPN or OT but sometimes a psychiatrist or psychologist, is appointed as the patient's keyworker. The keyworker remains in regular contact with the patient and their relatives or other carers and reviews the plan at intervals to make sure it is being carried out, and to make changes to the care plan when necessary.

The keyworker must send a copy of the patient's written care plan to all the professionals involved in a person's care, including their GP. Usually, the keyworker will also provide a copy of the care plan to the relatives or other carers, but this can only be done if the patient agrees, since it is confidential information.

The Care Programme Approach

- Assessment of a person's health and social needs
- Care planning meeting to which family or other carers should be invited
- Appointment of a keyworker(the first contact point for the patient and carer)

Care management

Care management refers to the process through which social service departments try to make sure that clients referred to them are assessed for social problems and have these problems addressed. A social service care manager usually has several clients for whom they have to purchase care. A care manager arranges for services to be provided but does not usually provide those services themselves.

Care management and the CPA should work hand-in-hand to provide for a person's social and medical needs. This does require that health and social service professionals meet at intervals to discuss a person's care.

Supervision registers

These were introduced in April 1994, to identify those people with severe mental illnesses such as schizophrenia who may be a significant risk to themselves or to others, and to ensure that local services focus effectively on these patients, who have the greatest needs for care and active follow-up. The local mental health service is responsible for taking steps to trace people on the supervision register who lose contact with services.

During the CPA planning meeting, usually before a person's discharge from hospital, a decision must be taken as to whether that person should be on the supervision register.

Patients likely to be put on the supervision register are those who

- may be a significant risk to themselves or others
- stop taking their medication
- misuse alcohol or drugs
- lack a supportive relationship (no family or close friends)
- lack suitable accommodation

To carry out the requirements of the supervision register, services will have to be preferentially targeted on those patients with the greatest likelihood of falling out of contact and becoming lost to follow-up by the mental health team.

Once again, the patient will be invited to the care planning meeting, along with their relatives or other carers if the patient agrees. The patient will be told what information about them will be kept on a supervision register, who else will know about their placement on the register (such as the GP for example), and why those people need to know that information.

The Patient's Charter

This was set up in 1991 to help improve services by informing people of their rights to health care, and the standards they should expect the NHS to meet. Copies of the Charter are available from hospitals, GP surgeries, chemists, and Community Health Councils.

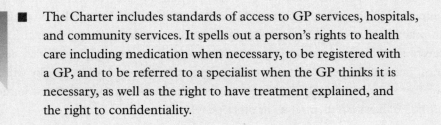

- The Charter includes standards of access to GP services, hospitals, and community services. It spells out a person's rights to health care including medication when necessary, to be registered with a GP, and to be referred to a specialist when the GP thinks it is necessary, as well as the right to have treatment explained, and the right to confidentiality.

Access to your own medical records

The Patient's Charter states that a person has the right to look at their own medical and other health records. However, in practice this is at the discretion of the doctors involved in a person's care and sometimes part of the medical record may be witheld and not shown to the patient. This is usually because the doctors consider that the patient may be harmed or seriously upset by reading something about themselves in their records. The GP or psychiatrist may use this discretion if they think that a patient with schizophrenia lacks insight into their problems and that it would lead to conflict and arguments if they read their own medical notes, which could damage their care.

Involving relatives and friends

The Charter states that, if a patient agrees, then they can expect their relatives and friends to be kept up to date with the progress of their treatment. In this way the Charter pays tribute to the idea of involving family and friends, but once again this can only be with the permission of the patient themselves, because they have a right to confidentiality.

The keyworker will usually be responsible for keeping relatives and friends up to date with a patient's progress.

The Charter and GP services

The Charter spells out the right to be registered with a GP (the Family Health Service Authority must find a doctor for you within two days) and the right to a health check on joining a practice and then every three years on request.

Patients on income support, family credit, or disability benefits, as well as people over sixty, are entitled to free prescriptions.

The Charter also states that GPs should provide leaflets about their services, to include all the arrangements listed above in the first section in this Chapter.

The Charter and hospital services

The Charter states that nine out of ten people can expect to be seen in the hospital outpatient clinic within thirteen weeks of being referred to a specialist by their GP. In practice, this would be a very long time for a person suffering from the more severe symptoms of schizophrenia to have to wait to see the psychiatrist, and in most parts of the country they would be seen much more quickly, usually within a week or two for seriously ill patients, and on the same day for patients at immediate risk of harming themselves or other people.

The Charter also states that you can expect to be given a specific appointment time, and to be seen in the outpatient clinic within thirty minutes of that time. In practice you may have to wait longer, for example if the psychiatrist or CPN is called out to see another patient in an emergency.

If you have to be admitted to hospital through the Casualty department (Accident and Emergency), the Charter states that you can expect to be found a bed in the hospital within four hours. Unfortunately, at the time of writing, experience suggests that this target is by no means always met in these days of reduced bed numbers in psychiatric hospital wards.

You should be told in advance if you are going into a ward with both men and women patients, and in any case you can expect to be provided with single-sex washing and toilet facilities.

The Charter and community services

The Charter states that you can expect the mental health nurse (CPN) to visit a patient:

- within four hours (in the daytime), if the person has been referred to the nurse as an urgent patient,
- within two working days, if the person has been referred as a non-urgent patient, and
- by appointment on the day you ask for, if you give the nurse more than 48 hours notice.

In practice, it may not be possible for the CPN always to come on the day you ask for, because most CPNs look after forty or so patients each and they have to get around to seeing all of them on a regular basis.

At the end of 1995, the Department of Health launched a framework for the development of *Local Community Care Charters*. The government wants health and social services in all parts of the country to get together and produce local charters with standards of access to care and waiting times which are written down.

Local authorities should

- include users and carers in the planning and assessment process
- respect users' personal beliefs
- show courtesy and respect at all times
- set standards for dealing with letters and enquiries
- protect personal information, and
- calculate charges for services (where relevant) fairly and accurately

This should provide an opportunity for patients and their families and friends to get involved in trying to improve the services offered in their local community.

How to complain

If you feel that something has gone wrong with a person's care, there are well laid down procedures for dealing with your complaint.

■ If you have a complaint with your GP, the first person to contact is the practice manager.

The practice manager will discuss the problem with the doctor concerned and give you a response to your complaint, usually within a few days unless the doctor is away on holiday. You may be invited to meet with the doctor concerned to discuss the complaint in more detail.

■ If you cannot sort the problem out with your own GP and practice manager, the next step is to contact your Family Health Service Authority (FHSA) or 'Primary Care Authority', which is the new name for the FHSA.

The telephone number is on your medical card, and in the telephone directory, or it can be obtained from your GP's practice. The Authority should acknowledge your complaint within two days, and sort out less serious complaints in a month. More serious complaints, such as those alleging a failure to provide proper medical care or those alleging professional misconduct, may take six months to deal with, and will usually involve a hearing to which the patient and their family or other carers will be invited.

■ Complaints about treatment or care in hospital should be addressed to the hospital General Manager or Chief Executive – the ward staff will inform patients and carers who to contact.

You can expect a response acknowledging your complaint within a few days, and eventually you should get a written reply which should fully address your complaint.

■ Your local *Community Health Council* is an independent source of help and advice on how to complain.

Their number is in the telephone book too, or you can obtain their address from your local GP or hospital.

■ If you are not satisfied with the answers to your complaints given by the FHSA or by a hospital, then you can ask the the *Health Service Commissioner for England*, also known as the *Ombudsman*, to consider investigating the complaint further.

The address is:

Health Service Commissioner for England
Church House
Great Smith Street,
London
SW1P 3BW.
Tel: 0171 217 4051.

■ The other source of help and advice is the *National Health Information Service*, which you can telephone free on: 0800 665 544.

6 The Mental Health Act and other legislation

Individual freedom versus making sure people get the treatment they need

Some might argue that it is wrong to put people in hospital and treat them against their will – that this takes away their basic human right to freedom. On the other hand, people suffering from schizophrenia sometimes don't realise that they are ill and need help. This is called *'loss of insight'*, and it may prevent sufferers getting the help they need. The Mental Health Act can be seen as society's way of making sure that mentally ill people get the necessary treatment to ease their problems, even when they can't see the need for it themselves. This is after all another basic right, the right to receive treatment for illness.

The 1983 Mental Health Act

The Act is divided into a number of 'Sections' which cover various different situations. (You may hear doctors or social workers using the term *'To section someone'*, which means using the Act to make sure the person goes to hospital for care).

In Scotland it is the Mental Health (Scotland) Act 1984, and in N. Ireland the Mental Health Order (N.I.) 1986 which apply.

Overall, Section 136 is the one most often applied, by the police. The Sections most frequently used by the psychiatrist, acting together with the person's GP, are Section 2 and Section 3. Section 4 may sometimes be used by the GP without involving a psychiatrist.

Section 136 – Mentally Disordered Persons Found in Public Places

This order authorises a police officer who finds a person who appears to be suffering from mental disorder, in a place to which the public has access, to remove the person to a *'place of safety'*. The officer may do so only if the person appears to be in immediate need of care and control, is in a public place (not in their own home), *and* the officer thinks it is necessary in the person's interest or for the protection of other people. The place of safety is usually a hospital, but might also be a police station, a residential home, or a nursing home.

The person may then be held at the place of safety for up to 72 hours in order to arrange, as soon as possible, for a medical examination by a psychiatrist and an interview with an *'Approved Social Worker'* (ASW). This is a social worker who has been specially trained and approved to apply the Sections of the Mental Health Act.

The possible results of the psychiatrist's and social worker's assessments are: release from the hospital or other place of safety, voluntary admission to hospital if the person agrees to go, or compulsory admission to hospital under another Section of the Act.

─── Section 2 – Admission for Assessment

This allows compulsory admission (holding the person against their will in hospital) for up to 28 days. The necessary grounds for using the Act are that the person is suffering from a mental disorder (such as schizophrenia) which is severe enough to need assessment in hospital, and that 'the person ought to be detained for their own health or safety or the protection of others'.

It is important to realise that detention may be justified in order to prevent a person's mental health getting any worse, which would obviously be harmful if nothing was done. The person's behaviour does not have to be immediately dangerous to themselves or others. They do not have to have attempted suicide or attacked anyone. The person may be at risk of coming to harm due to self-neglect, for example.

An application has to be made, on a special form, to the *'Hospital Managers'* (see below), for compulsory admission under the Act. This application may be made by the sufferer's *'nearest relative'*, (see below) but more often will be done by the ASW.

In Scotland the situation is covered by **Section 26 – Short Term Detention**. At the end of a 72-hour detention (under Section 24, similar to Section 4 in England), a person may be detained under Section 26 for a period of up to 28 days for reasons similar to those above.

The Mental Welfare Commission, the Local Authority – unless an MHO has already consented – and, where practicable, the nearest relative must all be informed of the patient's detention. There is a right of appeal to the Sheriff against detention.

In Northern Ireland, Article 4(2) of the Order applies. The nearest relative or social worker must make the application.

——— Duties of the Approved Social Worker or nearest relative

The applicant, whether it is the Approved Social Worker or the nearest relative, has to sign the form agreeing that *'I am satisfied that detention in a hospital is in all circumstances of the case the most appropriate way of providing the care and medical treatment of which the patient stands in need'*. It is better whenever possible for the social worker to make the application, to avoid the sufferer blaming the nearest relative for the admission, which could easily upset family relationships.

The nearest relative is, in order: the person's husband or wife (or common-law husband or wife if they have lived together for six months or more), the person's son or daughter, their mother or father, brother or sister, grandparent, grandchild, uncle or aunt, and nephew or niece. The eldest relative takes preference within a group. The relative must have seen the sufferer within the previous 14 days.

——— Duties of the doctors

As well as the application by the social worker or relative, the order requires the medical recommendation of two doctors. One doctor should be specially trained to apply the Act (this is usually the consultant psychiatrist) and the other doctor should if possible already know the person who is ill (this is usually the GP). They must have seen the patient within five days of signing the order.

If the person is willing to go into hospital voluntarily then the Mental Health Act should not apply. Doctors are taught that it is always better to persuade people to accept treatment and care voluntarily whenever possible, to avoid upsetting them and coming into conflict. However, in assessing the person's willingness to accept admission, the doctors and social worker will make a judgement about whether the person will stay in hospital or simply leave again immediately.

Section 2 is concerned with detaining people for assessment, but it also gives doctors the right to treat patients with medication for their mental illness.

The person may be detained for up to 28 days under Section 2. This period is not renewable and if a longer period of detention is thought by the doctors to be required then it may be followed by an application to apply Section 3 of the Act.

——— Section 3 – Admission for treatment

This Section allows the doctors to hold the person in hospital for up to six months for treatment, and is renewable in the first instance for another six months, and then after that for periods of one year each time it is renewed. Like Section 2, Section 3 requires an application by the Approved Social Worker or nearest relative, together with medical recommendations from two doctors, usually the consultant psychiatrist and the GP.

This procedure is covered in Scotland by Section 18 of the Mental Health (Scotland) Act 1984.

───── Section 4 – Emergency Admission for Assessment

This allows compulsory admission and detention for up to 72 hours for assessment only. It can be used by the applicant (Approved Social Worker or nearest relative) together with the person's GP, without a psychiatrist. It is designed only to be used in an emergency however, when those involved cannot cope with the person's mental state and they need to admit the person to hospital immediately, without having to wait to find a psychiatrist.

Section 4 cannot be renewed but it can be converted to a Section 2 (see above) on the recommendation of the psychiatrist once the person is in hospital. The person being admitted must be seen by the psychiatrist as soon as possible, and no later than 72 hours after admission.

This procedure is covered in Scotland by Section 24 of the above Act.

───── Compulsory treatment

In all cases, the psychiatrist must first offer treatment to the patient and ask for the person's consent to take it. If consent is not given, but the psychiatrist believes it is essential to treat the patient, then under Sections 2 and 3, treatment with medication can be given without the consent of the patient for up to three months. (This applies only to medication; treatment with electroconvulsive therapy (ECT) may only be given without the patient's consent after a second opinion from another consultant psychiatrist).

After three months, the psychiatrist must ask the patient once again to consent to further treatment with medication. If the patient does not give consent to treatment at this time, and the psychiatrist considers it essential, then once again the psychiatrist may arrange for a second opinion from another consultant psychiatrist. The appointment of this second psychiatrist is the job of an independent body, the *Mental Health Act Commission.*

───── The Mental Health Act Commission

This is a public body, a special health authority, made up of doctors, social workers, nurses, psychologists, lawyers, and lay people, which is responsible to the government for drawing up a *Code of Practice* for the Mental Health Act and for overseeing the facilities provided to detained patients. The Commission carries out official visits to hospitals and may interview detained patients and their relatives and hear any complaints they have. Their address and telephone number is:

Mental Health Act Commission
Maid Marian House, 56 Hounds Gate
Nottingham, NG1 6BG
Tel: 0115 943 7100

───── Ways of appealing against being held in hospital

The Mental Health Act Commission does not have the power to release detained patients. However, if a patient or the nearest relative disagrees with the doctor's order to be held in hospital, they can appeal.

As soon as possible after a person has been admitted to hospital under a Section of the Mental Health Act, they should be given written information (usually leaflets) about their rights whilst in hospital, and about the ways they may appeal against the Section if they wish.

There are two ways of challenging the Section. Appeals may be made to the *'Hospital Managers'*, or to the *'Mental Health Review Tribunal'*.

In Scotland, appeals can be made to the Sheriff's court, or to the Mental Welfare Commission for Scotland. Their address and telephone is:
Mental Welfare Commission for Scotland
25 Drumsheugh Gardens
Edinburgh EH3 7RN
Tel: 0131 225 7034

───── The Hospital Managers

The Hospital Managers involved in appeals against detention under the Mental Health Act are not the paid managers who work in the hospital but are lay people appointed by the local Health Authority. They are usually members of the local community who have an interest in the welfare of people who suffer from mental health problems.

Appealing against being Sectioned

- Appeals against detention under the Mental Health Act may be made to the Hospital Managers, or to a Mental Health Review Tribunal

Once the person detained has appealed, the Hospital Managers Appeal Panel should be assembled quickly. The patient will be told in writing of the day of the hearing, along with the patient's representative if they have one. This might be a relative, a friend, or possibly a lawyer (a solicitor). The consultant psychiatrist or other doctor, a social worker, and a senior member of the nursing staff who knows the person's case, will then present evidence to the appeal panel, after which the patient and their representative may also give their views and ask questions if they wish.

The Hospital Managers panel may decide that the person should be allowed to leave hospital, or that they must stay for the duration of the Section applied, or they may decide to refer the patient's case to a Mental Health Review Tribunal (see below). Whatever the decision, they will give it immediately after the appeal and the patient will be told the result on the same day, both through word of mouth and in writing.

——— The Mental Health Review Tribunal

This is an independent organisation set up by the government which acts like a 'mobile court'. The tribunal consists of three people – a lawyer, a doctor (a psychiatrist), and a third person who is not a doctor. All three people come from outside the hospital, and the hospital must give the patient the address of the tribunal so that the patient may appeal.

Mental Health Review Tribunal Offices

South East:
Mental Health Review Tribunal
Block 3
Crown Offices,
Kingston By-Pass Road
Surbiton,
Surrey KT6 5QN
Tel: 0181 268 4100

North West/East:
3rd Floor
Cressington House,
249 St Mary's Road
Garston
Liverpool
Merseyside L19 0NF
Tel: 0151 494 0095

London North:
Block 1
Spur 5
Canon's Park,
Government Buildings,
Honeypot Lane,
Stanmore
Middlesex HA7 1AY
Tel: 0171 972 3734

Midlands:
Spur A,
Block 5,
Government Buildings
Chalfont Drive
Western Boulevard,
Nottingham NG8 3RZ

Tel: 0115 929 4222.

In the case of Section 2 (the 28 day Section), the patient must make their appeal to the Tribunal within 14 days of the beginning of the order.

The tribunal will visit the hospital and ask to see the patient and the doctor. Again, a family member, a solicitor, or other supporter may also be present. The solicitor may be paid for through Legal Aid, which from April 1994 is available for all patients at Mental Health Review Tribunals, whatever their income. The Law Society publishes a list of solicitors approved to act in Tribunal cases. The list is available from:

The Law Society
Ipsley Court, Berrington Close,
Redditch, Worcestershire B98 0TD.
Tel: 0171 242 1222.

Mental Health Review Tribunal Offices continued	
Wales:	**N. Ireland**
1st Floor	Room 112B
New Crown Buildings,	Dundonald House
Cathay's Park	Upper Newtonards Road
Cardiff CF1 3NQ	Belfast BT4 35F
Tel: 01222 825328.	

The tribunal may decide that the person should be discharged from hospital, or that they should be allowed a period of leave away from the hospital, or be transferred to another hospital.

Any patient who has been detained under Section 3 for six months and who has not applied to a Mental Health Review Tribunal **must** be referred to a Tribunal by the Hospital Managers.

Other Sections of the Mental Health Act

Other Sections you may hear mentioned are as follows:

SECTION 5(2)

Detention of a patient already in hospital who wishes to leave against the doctors' advice. This is a temporary order by the hospital doctor. It lasts for 72 hours, after which the patient may leave unless Section 2 or 3 has been applied.

SECTION 5(4)

This is a similar temporary holding order to Section 5(2), but is applied by a senior nurse in the hospital and lasts for only five hours unless another Section is then applied.

In Scotland, Section 25(2) allows a fully qualified nurse to detain an informal patient for up to two hours or until the earlier arrival of a doctor, if it seems the patient needs to be restrained from leaving hospital for his own health or safety, or for the protection of others. This period cannot be extended.

In N. Ireland, under the same circumstances, a nurse may hold a patient for no more than six hours, or until the arrival of a doctor if that is sooner.

SECTIONS 35, 36, 37, 38, AND 41.

These Sections may be applied by the Crown Court or Magistrates Court, when the courts decide a person who has been arrested by the police ought to be detained in hospital for care or treatment of a mental illness, rather than go to prison.

In each case, the person detained in hospital under the Mental Health Act should be given written information about the Section under which they are being held, and about how they may appeal against it.

Legislation concerned with Care in the Community

The Sections of the Mental Health Act described above are all concerned with detention in hospital. In these days of more provision of care in the community, a number of legal developments mean that some patients may be subject to certain restrictions and supervision after they leave hospital.

Section 117 – After-care

■ In the case of patients held in hospital under Section 3 (as well as some of the other Sections applied by the courts), the Mental Health Act, Section 117, requires the Health Authority and the Local Authority Social Services between them to provide care after the person's discharge from hospital, to last until the authorities are satisfied that this is no longer necessary.

This means that a meeting must be held of all the professionals involved with the person's case, before they are discharged from hospital, to plan their future care. This will involve drawing up a programme of treatment and allocating a key worker, which should be the case now anyway for all patients looked after by the mental health services, under the *Care Programme Approach* (see Chapter 5). The difference under Section 117 is that the authorities are obliged by law to hold such a care planning meeting, to which all the professionals involved in a person's care must be invited.

The Section 117 care plan may include advising the patient where they will be expected to live, (perhaps in an after-care hostel or group home rather than living on their own), and how often they should see their key worker. The patient will usually have to consent to the plan before they are allowed to leave hospital.

Supervised discharge

Since April 1996, under the Mental Health (Patients in the Community) Act, supervised discharge has been introduced for certain patients who have been detained under the Mental Health Act 1983.

■ Supervised discharge is designed to help those patients who go through repeated cycles of admission to hospital followed by a breakdown in arrangements for their care in the community and rapid readmission to hospital.

This happens sometimes, usually because the patient stops taking medication and drops out of contact with their key worker. These unfortunate patients have become known as 'revolving door' patients and need extra help and supervision of their care.

A patient subject to supervised discharge must abide by the care plan drawn up before they leave hospital, at the Section 117 meeting. A supervisor – who will in most cases also be the person's key worker – will be appointed with powers to:

■ require the patient to live in a specified place

■ require the patient to attend for medical treatment

■ take the person to the place where they are to attend for such treatment.

If the patient fails to go along with the plan for their accommodation and treatment after hospital discharge then under the supervised discharge laws they may be readmitted compulsorily back into hospital. Supervised discharge applies for six months to begin with, after which time it could be applied for another six months, and then for 12 month periods after that. Patients have the right to appeal to the Mental Health Review Tribunal against supervised discharge being imposed on them.

People subject to supervised discharge will also be included on the mental health service's supervision register (see Chapter 7), so that their needs are given priority when services are being planned. The difference for patients under supervised discharge is that they can be taken back to hospital again if the doctors, nurses, and social workers who are looking after them consider it necessary for their care.

━━━━━ Guardianship

In Scotland and N. Ireland, a patient over 16 years of age may be 'received into guardianship'. This requires an application similar to the 518 application for admission to be made to the Sheriff by the nearest relative or the Mental Health Officer. In N. Ireland the application must be supported by two medical recommendations and one from a social worker. The guardian (who will be either the Local Authority or a person chosen or accepted by the Local Authority) must be named. The guardian can specify where the patient shall live, places he shall go for treatment, occupation, education or training, and require that access be given to a doctor, MHO or other person.

━━━━━

The working of the new Mental Health (Patients in the Community) Act in England and Wales will be subject to a written Code of Practice drawn up by the Mental Health Act Commission, whose address is on page 44. If patients or their families or friends have complaints or comments to make about how the laws are working, they should not feel afraid to make their views known by writing to the Commission.

It is unfortunate that laws have to be passed which in a way restrict the freedom of people suffering from illnesses like schizophrenia. However, the present day legislation is a big improvement on past legislation, when patients could be held in hospital for long periods without an appeal.

Every effort is made to keep patients out of hospital, but that does mean that the doctors and social workers responsible for helping patients in the community do sometimes need the power to insist that patients continue with their care and treatment. If only people with schizophrenia always realised when they needed care. Unfortunately for some, they turn away from help just when they need it most. Maybe in the future better treatment will be developed which will quickly help people to regain their insight into their own needs for care. Until that day, some laws will be necessary for society to make sure that vulnerable people suffering from mental illnesses get the care they need even when they themselves do not see the need for it.

> Note: The information regarding the Mental Health Acts given here is necessarily abbreviated and more specific detail in any particular case should be sought from an appropriate legal body or a specialist voluntary advice line
> (see Chapter 8 and Appendix).

7 Complications of schizophrenia: suicide and violence

Sometimes, reading the papers or listening to the news, you could almost be forgiven for thinking that people with schizophrenia are all unpredictable and dangerous and should be locked away for their own and everyone else's good. Of course, the reality is that the large majority – nine out of ten people with schizophrenia – do not hurt themselves or others. When suicide or violence does occur, then obviously everyone gets very concerned and the press is obliged to report what has happened. That is why most people without personal experience of schizophrenia hear only about the violent or self-destructive behaviour of some sufferers.

> ■ **Nine out of ten people with schizophrenia do not try to hurt themselves or others**

There are reasons why some people suffering from schizophrenia become desperate and consider suicide, and also reasons why some can become frightened and hostile or even violent towards others. Violence is sometimes directed at the person's family or other carers, the very people who are providing most support to the sufferer. On rare occasions violence may be directed at complete strangers. However, usually these situations do not just happen out of the blue – they are to an extent predictable and may be prevented by adequate care and supervision.

People with schizophrenia are at risk of becoming depressed, and it is usually this depression which leads some to try and end their lives. Sometimes depression comes just after the person has recovered from a breakdown of their schizophrenia, and is no longer suffering from the most severe symptoms such as hallucinations or delusions (see Chapter 1). Perhaps the person has just left hospital. It may be difficult to come to terms with the realisation of how ill they have been, and what has happened to their lives during their stay in hospital.

Those suffering from schizophrenia may feel guilty about how they have behaved whilst they were really ill, or feel that they have let their family or friends down. They may feel anxious about developing another bout of schizophrenia. They may grieve for the job they have lost, the qualifications they failed to get, or the girlfriend or boyfriend who has left them, because of their illness. All their hopes and expectations for their lives may have to change. It is not surprising then that depression is common among people with schizophrenia.

———— Recognising depression

When people get depressed, they may look low and unhappy, they may cry, and they may say how depressed they feel. On the other hand, this is not always the case, and some people can be feeling suicidal inside, yet on the surface they may seem calm or even happy. Often, however, their behaviour will have changed in some way.

Their pattern of sleep may change, with frequent waking up and less sleep, or sometimes sleeping more than usual. They may lose their appetite and lose weight, or on the other hand they may eat more than usual and gain weight. They may be anxious, restless, and unable to sit still, or they may become slowed down in their movements and very inactive. People who are depressed will almost certainly stop enjoying the things in life that used to give them pleasure, like hobbies, sports, or seeing friends.

People who are depressed often neglect themselves, lose their self-esteem, and stop looking after their appearance and their home. They may become irritable and unfriendly and impatient, and put other people off helping them. Such behaviour then increases the person's loneliness and isolation and in turn makes them more depressed, in a vicious circle.

Possible changes in someone who is getting depressed

- Looking miserable and unhappy, or crying (not always)
- Losing interest and enjoyment in the nice things in life
- Changes in sleep pattern, sleeping more or sleeping less
- Changes in appetite and weight, going up or going down
- Changes in level of activity, either being unable to keep still, or slowing right down
- Irritability, impatience, and complaining more than usual
- Loss of self-esteem, feeling very guilty or unworthy of help
- Keeping themselves to themselves, withdrawal, isolation
- Self-neglect, poor hygiene, neglecting the home
- Drinking more alcohol

Some people try to relieve their feelings of depression by drinking more alcohol than usual. This may make them feel better whilst they are drinking, because they feel they can escape from the cares of the world. Unfortunately, drinking more alcohol ends up making a person more depressed when the good feelings have worn off. In the long term, alcohol leads to an increased risk of more serious depression, and suicide may be more likely when the person is drunk. The same may be true of abusing drugs.

It is important, if you suspect a person is becoming depressed, that you try to get them to see a doctor or other professional, because psychological support or anti-depressant treatment can often help. If untreated, depression may get so bad that the person becomes desperate, sees no way out and no future for themselves, and begins to contemplate suicide.

How to predict suicide

Research studies have found that suicide in people with schizophrenia is more likely in some groups of patients than others. On the basis of such research, doctors and nurses are taught that the risk of suicide is greater in younger patients, in men more than women, among single more than among married people, among people who have previously had a death from suicide in their family, among those who drink a lot of alcohol or abuse drugs, and among those who have recently been discharged from hospital.

These so-called 'risk factors' are not very helpful in predicting suicide in any one person's case, however, because they are only a guide to a possible increase in risk in a particular group of people. Even among young single men with schizophrenia who drink a lot of alcohol, have a family history of suicide, and have recently come out of hospital, the large majority do **not** commit suicide, although they have a statistically increased risk.

Risk factors for suicide in schizophrenia

The risk is definitely greater if:
- the person is depressed
- the person has tried to commit suicide before
- they have recently been bereaved, or suffered some other major
- upset or severe stress
- they keep talking about ending their life
- they seem to have no hope for the future
- they suddenly make a will
- they start to write suicide notes

Some groups are generally more at risk:
- single young men
- those recently discharged from hospital
- those who drink too much alcohol, or abuse drugs
- those with a family history of suicide

Some risk factors are more useful in an individual person's case however. Those people who have previously tried to commit suicide are at a considerably greater risk of trying again. This is true even if the previous suicide attempt didn't seem to be very serious, or if the person seemed to know that they would be found out and prevented from going through with it. Those who talk about killing themselves are more at risk of one day going through with it, even though sometimes it may seem like an idle threat which people use to get their own way. People who continually state that everything is hopeless and there is no point in trying to go on are also at greater risk. Those who have recently been bereaved or had a major upset or trauma in their life are also at increased risk. Those who go so far as to suddenly write a will or who start to write suicide notes must be considered as very vulnerable and every effort should be made to get them to see a their general practitioner, psychiatrist, or community psychiatric nurse.

─────── GETTING HELP

- ■ For those people who are in contact with a psychiatrist or a community psychiatric nurse, it is important that depression and any hint of suicidal ideas are brought to the attention of the professionals.
- ■ For those people who are not in contact with these psychiatric services, it is important that the problem is brought to the attention of the person's general practitioner.

There is evidence that many people who commit suicide go to see their general practitioner more frequently in the weeks leading up to their death. It seems that they are looking for help. Unfortunately, they do not always find it easy to let their doctor know how depressed they have become. Even when a person is feeling suicidal they may feel they should put on a brave face for the world. They may be so depressed that they can't think straight and so don't get across to the doctor how bad they feel. Having someone go to see the doctor with them who knows how they have been feeling can be tremendously helpful. It may help to write things down so as not to forget to mention them when in the doctor's surgery. The doctor will usually go through each point and answer each question carefully when asked.

When doctors do detect depression, in most cases it is treatable with psychological support, or with antidepressants. Antidepressants are not like tranquillisers (such as Valium) which can sometimes just make people drowsy and stop them thinking clearly. Antidepressants are not addictive, and can be stopped easily once they have worked to relieve the symptoms of depression, usually after four to six months.

If antidepressants are prescribed, then ideally the bottle of pills should be kept by the person's family or other carers, and the pills given to the sufferer under supervision, to prevent them taking an overdose, which can be fatal.

Sometimes, the person is so desperate, so sure that they must end their life, or that they do not deserve to live, that they refuse to see a doctor or to accept that they need help. If the person is seriously suicidal and won't accept help, they may have to be admitted compulsorily under a section of the Mental Health Act (see Chapter 6).

Violent behaviour

Most violent behaviour by people with schizophrenia is unplanned, done on the spur of the moment, often without thinking through the consequences, and usually very much regretted by the perpetrator after the event. Many of us have behaved like this at times – you don't have to have schizophrenia.

The same factors which increase the risk of self-harm can also increase the risk of someone with schizophrenia hitting out at someone else, often the people nearest to them, their family or other carers. Anxiety and depression may lead to irritability, hostility, and violence at times. Certain groups of people with schizophrenia are more likely to be violent, namely young single men, especially those who misuse alcohol or drugs, those who have been under severe stress, and especially where there is a past history of violence. This is also true of many young men in the general population, and it should be remembered that only a small proportion of violent acts are committed by people with schizophrenia.

Things which increase the risk of violence

- Young, single, male sex
- Anxious, depressed, and irritable
- Recent bad experiences or severe stress
- Alcohol or drug misuse
- A past history of previous violence
- Development of delusions of persecution

There is, however, one situation which, whilst uncommon, can be particularly dangerous in schizophrenia, and has led to tragedies including the killing of complete strangers. This is the development of a delusion, a false belief, by the person with schizophrenia that someone else is out to hurt them, trying to control them in some way, or even out to kill them. This delusion of persecution obviously only happens when the person is very ill and cannot see that the belief is false. In this situation the person may strike first in the belief that they are preventing themselves from being hurt or killed by whoever they think is out to harm them.

Because of this, it is very important to take it seriously when a person with schizophrenia says that someone else is trying to control them, dominate them, or hurt them in some way. With professional help, perhaps through increased drug treatment, such a delusion can often be completely removed or at least reduced in strength of feeling, and the person will then no longer be dangerous.

——— Lack of care and supervision

The most dangerous situation arises when someone with schizophrenia has such delusions of persecution but is receiving no care, monitoring, or supervision by the professionals, the doctors and nurses who really do need to keep in contact. The well-publicised tragedies ending in killing have usually occurred in situations where the person has lost all contact with professional help, and no one is taking responsibility for helping them to get the treatment they need. This can be difficult of course, because by its nature the illness affects the person's own ability to recognise that they need help; insight into their own condition is often lacking just when they need help most. This is why the government has introduced the Supervision Register to make sure that those patients most at risk of hurting themselves or others receive extra help and supervision (see Chapter 6).

A dangerous situation

- The person with schizophrenia believes someone is out to hurt them and can't be persuaded it's not true
- The person says they are going to hurt another person in a particular way, and perhaps gets hold of a weapon
- The person is not receiving care or supervision by the mental health services

——— GETTING HELP

- If a person has been violent previously, whilst suffering from a breakdown in their schizophrenia, it is very important to seek help early if the person starts to behave in a way which might be the early signs of a further breakdown, known as a relapse.

This might be a change in their sleep pattern, or signs that they are becoming anxious or irritable, or odd behaviours – perhaps saying strange things or hearing voices. When a person has had more than one previous breakdown then it is often obvious to the family or other carers when another breakdown is starting to happen.

■ It is particularly important to get more help and treatment for a person who is talking about harming someone else, particularly if they seem to be planning some specific action or are gathering weapons to use.

The risk should be assessed by a professional, preferably a psychiatrist or community psychiatric nurse. If the person is in contact with the psychiatric services then the family or other carers should have the telephone number of the key worker assigned to the sufferer under the Care Programme Approach (see Chapter 6). This is the first line of contact.

Getting more help may need referral by the GP for someone who is not in contact with the mental health services. If someone does not have a GP, is not known to the mental health services, and refuses to go and sign on with a doctor, or go to the hospital, then the police may have to become involved. It is important that someone takes responsibility for making sure that action is taken. Sometimes the person's family or other carers might have to keep insisting that a doctor or other professional assesses the person and assesses the risk of violence. It is vital that the professionals assessing the sufferer have all the information that the carers can provide to give them the complete picture.

When actually faced with violent behaviour, it helps, if you can, to remain as calm as possible, try not to react by shouting back or hitting back at the violent person, sympathise with the way that they must be feeling, but tell them that their behaviour is frightening you, and leave as soon as possible. Try to avoid being trapped; try to keep between the violent person and the door so that you can get out. Don't take any chances, but leave sooner rather than later, particularly if there are young children in a house where someone is being aggressive or violent.

How to help someone who does not want treatment

It is difficult to help someone who refuses to accept that they need treatment and won't see a doctor or nurse or social worker or other professional. However, often something can be done. The person might accept treatment from their own GP, especially if they have known that doctor for some years. Even if they refuse to see a psychiatrist, the GP might be able to start treatment after discussion of the person's case with a specialist over the telephone. It may help not to use the words schizophrenia, psychosis, or even mental illness, if the person suffering it refuses to accept the idea. However, they might accept drug treatment on the basis that it will help them to sleep and to feel calmer. If the person poses no risk to themselves or others, and their health is not deteriorating to the point where they are neglecting themselves, then it is reasonable to wait and to try repeatedly but gently to get the person to see the doctor or to accept some treatment. It is important in such a situation to avoid pressurising the person, because they may react against the idea and become even more difficult to help. It is not a good idea to trick the person into seeing a psychiatrist by telling them or allowing them to believe that they are seeing some other sort of specialist. When they realise they have been tricked they are likely to be suspicious of any further attempts to help them.

If the person seems to be seriously suicidal, or their behaviour poses a threat to others, and they refuse to seek help, then they may have to be admitted to hospital compulsorily under a section of the Mental Health Act (see Chapter 6). This should always be avoided where possible, but should be used where really necessary, so that the person can get the help they need. In an ideal world, where enough services are provided in hospitals and in the community, every person suffering from schizophrenia should be able to get the treatment they need, which should prevent acts of suicide and violence which no one, least of all the sufferer themselves, wants ever to happen.

8 Helping carers

Carers' groups and support networks

Those who care for relatives or friends with schizophrenia are not alone. In many parts of the country, carers have come together to form groups which meet from time to time, to give each other support, advice, and information. There may be such a group already in existence in your district. If so, the community psychiatric nurse, social worker, psychiatrist, or GP should be able to put you in touch with the group. If such a group does not already exist in your area, you might consider starting one up, if you feel energetic enough and you can enlist the help of other carers.

Support, advice, and information

The aims of carers' groups usually include support, which may be sympathy and encouragement expressed in a group meeting, or one-to-one conversations with another carer who has been through the same sorts of difficulties. Some carers remain available to each other for late-night calls for help with their relatives with schizophrenia.

Advice from another carer with similar problems is often extremely valuable, as they have 'been there' themselves. Carers can advise each other about what to do when the person with schizophrenia is showing difficult behaviour such as aggression, bizarre or embarrassing behaviour, or staying up all night, and won't listen.

Information is also a valuable part of carers' groups. Details of day centres, employment schemes, accommodation, and respite care may be known to the more experienced carers and can be quickly passed on to the less experienced.

Helping sufferers to stay well

Carers can best help themselves by helping their relatives or friends with schizophrenia to stay well. To remind you, this can best be done in the following ways:

ENCOURAGING THE PERSON TO TAKE THEIR MEDICATION

The chances of a person with schizophrenia suffering a worsening of their illness, or another severe episode (a 'relapse') are more than halved in most cases if the person continues to take medication long-term (see Chapter 3). The carer may be best placed to make sure the person takes the medication.

Sometimes the medication causes the person side-effects, such as drowsiness, odd movement difficulties, restlessness, and other effects (see Chapter 3), and the person may wish to stop taking it. In these circumstances it is important for the GP, CPN, or psychiatrist to be consulted, as there are usually things which can be done to relieve side-effects without stopping the medication. Stopping it could well cause a relapse.

■ **Medication should not be stopped without discussion with the doctor.**

AVOIDING CRITICISM OR OVER-INVOLVEMENT

As discussed in Chapter 2, people with schizophrenia often need some space and time alone, and may find it hard to play a full role in family life. Criticising the person for 'laziness', or trying too hard to get the person to take part in family activities, may actually put too much pressure on the person and increase the risk of a relapse. It is best to avoid too much 'expressed emotion' (see Chapter 2), which includes critical comments but also over-protectiveness and expectations of frequent contact, which may be perceived by the sufferer as 'smothering'.

■ **Avoid too much expressed emotion**

STAYING SANE ONESELF

It's very important for someone faced with caring for a person with schizophrenia to look after themselves too, as the job may go on for some years. Giving yourself time and space is important too. Adequate respite will help to guard against becoming exhausted and depressed and unsympathetic. Ideally respite breaks from caring should be available for several hours each week, as well as for the occasional break for a holiday of one or two weeks as a block.

Saying 'no' is likely to be necessary sometimes, as we all have to live within the limits of the tolerance of others around us. The person with schizophrenia may behave in ways which would be intolerable, and this behaviour needs to be addressed, and limits set, with help from the community psychiatric nurse, social worker, or doctor. Day centres and day hospitals should be provided in every district. If day care and other forms of respite are not available then it may be necessary for carers to campaign for it to be introduced – another function of carers' groups.

Remember also, if you have a son or daughter with the illness, whatever causes schizophrenia, one thing is certain – *the illness is not your fault !*

Staying sane yourself

- Give yourself space and time to relax
- Find out about respite care, on a weekly basis as well as for holiday cover
- Learn to say no when necessary
- Seek professional help in setting limits on difficult behaviour
- Remember – the illness is not your fault!

Voluntary organisations which can help

MIND

MIND, the National Association for Mental Health, was set up in 1946. It is a charitable organisation run by volunteers (many of them carers or ex-carers of people with schizophrenia) and funded mainly by donations, subscriptions, charity shops, and sponsored events.

MIND campaigns for a better life for people diagnosed, 'labelled' or treated as mentally ill, and for their right to lead an active and valued life in the community. The organisation stresses the rights of sufferers and sometimes finds itself in opposition to doctors and other professional groups, especially over issues like electro-convulsive therapy (ECT) to which some people have strong objections. MIND especially stresses the needs of black people, women, and other groups it regards as particularly vulnerable or oppressed.

MIND can help carers by putting them in touch with a network of supporters throughout England and Wales.

MIND services

Relatives' support schemes	Legal help
Counselling	Education
Crisis help-lines	Publishing
Employment projects	Mental health bookshops
Training schemes	Special needs housing
Drop-in centres	Day centres
Befriending	Advocacy

Legal help from MIND includes advice and guidance from a network of more than 600 lawyers in England and Wales. MIND has represented some sufferers and carers in court, in some selected test cases.

Educational activities of MIND include courses, 'workshops', and conferences. (A workshop is a group meeting in which the group members address specific tasks rather than simply having a speaker talk to them).

MIND publishes books and leaflets on mental illness and its treatment, legal issues, benefits and employment, community care, racial and gender issues, the special problems of young people, making wills, and dealing with death. Contact MIND publications on 0181-519-2122.

> ■ For general information, contact MIND through its INFO-LINE on 0345 660 163 (local call rates), or on 0181 522 1728 in London.

The address of the national office is:
MIND
Granta House
15-17 Broadway
London
E15 4BQ.

There are also regional offices in the North, North-West, South-East, South-West, West Midlands, Trent & Yorkshire, and Wales.

─── The National Schizophrenia Fellowship (NSF)

This was founded by a carer, John Pringle, in 1972. It is a national organisation for all matters concerning people with experience of schizophrenia and their families, carers, and dependants. The NSF has a network of more than 160 local community self-help groups, all made up of carers themselves.

The fellowship is a charity, funded from grants and donations, fundraising activities, members' subscriptions, and Local Authority (Council) and Health Authority contracts for services performed.

NSF services

Housing projects	Day care projects
Befriending	Family support
Training courses for professionals	Expert conferences
Advice and information	Holidays
Quarterly members' newsletter	Books and leaflets

The NSF wants the current programme of hospital closures to be slowed right down until more community services can be provided to take the place of the hospitals. It wants more trained social workers and community psychiatric nurses, and more small domestic-style community homes built.

The fellowship provides advice on the care and treatment of schizophrenia, hospital admissions, welfare benefits, how to make or change a will or a covenant, accommodation available, family problems, and holiday breaks.

The NSF runs one-day training courses for social workers, community psychiatric nurses, the police, the probation service, psychiatrists, and GPs.

Books and leaflets available from the NSF cover the illness, its symptoms, treatment, and the provision of care and support services, with such titles as:

Care and Aftercare, Cognitive Therapy, Disability Living Allowance, Finding the Right Medication, Sulpiride, Risperidone, Clozapine, Notes on Wills and Trusts, Psychiatric Diagnosis, Silent Partners – the needs and experiences of people who care for people with a severe mental illness, Sudden Death, and *What is Schizophrenia?*

The address of the head office is:
National Schizophrenia Fellowship
28 Castle Street
Kingston-on-Thames
Surrey
KT1 1SS
Tel: 0181 547 3937.

There are also regional offices in Central London, Southampton, West Bromwich, Bridgend, Exeter, Belfast, and Maidstone.

■ The NSF Advice Line is: 0181 974 6814 and is open from Monday to Friday between 10 am and 3 pm.

——— Voices

Voices is one of the services funded by the NSF, together with SANE (see below). Voices is a service aimed at advising and supporting sufferers of schizophrenia themselves.

——— SANE

SANE stands for Schizophrenia – A National Emergency. It was started in 1986, following the campaign by Marjorie Wallace in *The Times* called 'The Forgotten Illness'. The organisation has three main aims:

INCREASING AWARENESS OF THE PROBLEMS OF PEOPLE WITH SCHIZOPHRENIA

This is achieved through public awareness campaigns in the media, and by lobbying MPs.

INFORMATION AND SUPPORT TO SUFFERERS AND CARERS

The 'SANELINE' service is a telephone crisis line which takes calls every day of the year between the hours of 2 pm and 12 midnight. It is manned by volunteers who have been trained to listen to people's problems and give advice, counselling, and information on sources of available help.

> ■ The telephone number for SANELINE is 0345 678 000
> (local call rates)

As well as the crisis line, SANE funds **Voices** together with the NSF, and also funds the Sturt Enterprise for Sheltered Employment.

SANE, like MIND and the NSF, also runs a Legal Information Service, and publishes regular newsletters.

RESEARCH

SANE also funds research into the causes of mental illness, and has given over £400,000 in grants.

Conclusion

> ■ If you are caring for someone with schizophrenia and finding it hard
> going, maybe even feeling desperate and suicidal yourself, please
> don't despair, give someone a ring now, either your own family
> doctor, community psychiatric nurse, or social worker, or if you
> don't know where to turn, ring one of these voluntary organisations
> now. Lots can be done to make your task easier – you are not alone!

Some commonly used words and phrases explained

Akathisia – a distressing side effect of drug treatment, which is a sensation of inner and muscular tension and can be mistaken for the agitation of acute illness with restlessness, pacing, and repeated sitting and standing.

Antipsychotic drugs – drugs which control symptoms of schizophrenia, usually long-term, and other serious mental illnesses. (Also known as **major tranquillisers** and **neuroleptic drugs.**)

Anxiety management – psychological techniques based on 'talking and doing' methods aimed at helping people control anxiety symptoms using eg. deep breathing, relaxation exercises, distraction, and graded exposure to feared situations.

Care at home – people who are not too ill can be treated at home and visit hospital as an outpatient.

Care in the community – local health and social services assess what a person's needs are and give help that takes account of religious, cultural or language needs.

Care plan – a plan which addresses a person's social, medical and nursing needs, it is drawn up as part of the Care Plan Approach.

Care programme approach (CPA) – professionals from health services and the local authority arrange care together. The CPA applies to patients accepted for care by the specialist mental health services.

Chronic/acute/sub-acute – refer to lengths of illness, the term acute can also mean severe.

Clinical psychologists – encourage patients to talk about feelings and worries and help to work out a plan of action so patients can understand the reasons for problems and do something positive about them.

Cognitive therapy – (also called cognitive-behavioural therapy) is a short-term 'talking and doing' treatment that uses collaboration between therapist and patient to alter unwanted patterns of thinking and behaving. The techniques used include identifying and studying unwanted thought processes, scheduling activities using diaries, increasing a sense of mastery and pleasure from activities, tackling tasks and problems in a graded fashion, and rehearsing new patterns of thinking and behaviour.

Commission for Racial Equality – helps individuals with cases of racial discrimination, investigates incidences of discrimination and works to promote good race relations. Their telephone number is 0171 828 7022.

Community mental health centre – a local base in the community where patients meet members of the mental health team.

Community mental health nurses – have experience of working in hospitals as well as in the community and can administer medication or injections, provide 'talking' treatments and long-term support.

Community mental health team – a group of mental health professionals, (eg. doctors nurses, psychologists, social workers, occupational therapists, therapists and support nurses) based in the community and who are responsible for caring, helping and treating patients in the community.

Day centres – give continued support and help people prepare for everyday life.

Day hospitals – a person can be admitted to day hospital to receive treatment and support and return home at the end of each day.

Delusion – a false belief out of keeping with reality and with the shared beliefs of the person's background and culture.

Delusions of grandeur – a belief in self-importance, greatness or superiority, eg a person may believe he or she can do anything – break sports records at will, influence people by telepathy, have fabulous wealth.

Delusion of persecution – belief in victimisation by one or more individuals or groups, eg.by the IRA, CIA or Masonic Lodges.

Depot injections – deep muscle injections containing drugs that are slowly released into the body and are particularly useful for people who usually forget or who are reluctant to take tablets regularly.

Drop-in centres – give people a chance to meet others with similar problems.

ECT (electro-convulsive therapy) sounds dramatic but is a safe hospital treatment which can help people to recover quickly. It is seldom used for people with schizophrenia except when they are either in a stupor or in a state of great agitation and excitement and dangerously ill through exhaustion and not eating or drinking,or when they have severe depressive illness.

Expressed emotion (also known as EE) – includes critical remarks and hostility towards the sufferer, but also expressions of emotional over-involvement, with over-protectiveness.

Extrapyramidal side effects – stiffness and trembling, like in Parkinson's disease. These occur in about a third of patients on traditional antipsychotic medication and can be treated with anti-parkinsonian drugs.

General practitioner – the main person responsible for caring and day-to-day treatment, usually involved in crises and in referral for specialist treatment.

Group homes/flatlets – offer a chance to people discharged from hospital to live with friends, or people they met in hospital.

Group/family therapy – these therapies are aimed at the group or family unit rather than the individual. The unit is seen as not working properly and techniques are aimed at helping the group or family as a whole to function better. No one is blamed for the situation and all are able to contribute to find solutions to improve communication and behaviour patterns.

Hallucination – a sensation or perception when there is nothing there to account for it, for example hearing voices or seeing visions.

Health Information Service – a national network designed to help callers make better use of NHS services. It is a confidential information service and gives personal counselling and will provide details of sources of help. Their telephone number is 0800 665544.

Key worker – a health or mental health worker appointed to act as the link between patients and other mental health workers to coordinate a persons care package. They will talk to patients, carers and all those involved to make sure that the care plan is working out.

Mental Health Act (1983)- an Act of Parliment which is divided into a number of 'Sections' which cover various different situations.The Act ensures that mentally ill people get the necessary treatment to ease their problems, even when they can't see the need for it themselves. Chapter 6 gives further details.

Mental Health Act Commission – is a Special Health Authority which consists of lawyers, doctors, nurses, lay people and their main function is to review use of the Mental Health Act. They investigate complaints and can interview patients under the Act in hospitals and mental nursing homes.Their telephone number is 0115 943 7100.

MIND – is a national organisation working for a better life for people diagnosed as having mental illness. Their telephone number is 0345 660 163 (local call rates) or 0181 522 1728 in London.

National Schizophrenia Fellowship – is a national organisation which provides information and services for those suffering from schizophrenia and their relatives, friends and carers. Their telephone number is 0181 547 3937.

Negative symptoms (of schizophrenia)- these include blunted emotions, lack of interest and energy, apathy and social withdrawal.

Neuroleptic drugs – drugs which control symptoms of schizophrenia and other, usually long-term, mental illness (also known as **major tranquillisers** and **antipsychotic drugs**)

Non-compliance (also known as treatment non-adherence) – not taking medication at the correct time, at the correct dose, or at all.

Nursing homes – provide patients with support and care in a homely environment.

Occupational therapists – trained to help patients develop confidence and practical skills for living independently, eg shopping or cooking. They use creative activities, eg dance and music, to help to release tension and increase self-expression.

Positive symptoms – these include hallucinations, delusions, disturbance of thought processes as shown by incoherent speech, being illogical, etc. and bizarre patterns of behaviour.

Psychiatrists – medically trained doctors specially trained to diagnose mental and physical illness and to prescribe treatment. They work closely with other professionals in community mental health teams.

Relapse – this is a return of symptoms of illness occurring during a period of remission from illness (see below)

Remission – a relatively brief period during which a person who has been ill has no symptoms.

Residential care homes – provide people with a supportive environment with trained staff.

Respite care/crisis unit – patients can be admitted to an acute psychiatric unit for a short stay if particularly unwell or to give relatives and carers a break during a crisis.

The Samaritans – offers confidential counselling to everyone passing through a difficult period of personal crisis and at risk of taking their own lives. Their telephone number is 01753 532713.

SANE – provides care, awareness and research in schizophrenia and other mental health illnesses. It has a comprehensive database of organisations and self-help groups and can refer enquirers to local services. SANELINE operates a helpline for 365 days of the year. The SANELINE telephone number is 0345 678 000.

Social workers – can assess people's needs in the community and try to ensure that these are met. They provide people with care and help to deal with the problems of everyday living as well as problems within families. Specialist mental health social workers are called Approved Social Workers.

Supervision Register – taking account of the views of all concerned, a consultant psychiatrist who considers a person to be at significant risk of suicide, self-neglect, or injury or of seriously harming other people, can place the patient's name on the Supervision Register. The idea is to help local health and social services make sure that particularly vulnerable or needy patients are given the care they need and to keep a close check on their progress.

Voluntary groups – work alongside services locally providing care and support for people with mental illness.

Waxy flexibility – a person maintains limbs and body in positions another person has placed them in.

The authors

PROFESSOR GREG WILKINSON graduated in Medicine at Edinburgh University and trained as a psychiatrist at the Maudsley Hospital in London. He is Professor of Liaison Psychiatry at the University of Liverpool where he has responsibility for patient care, teaching medical students and undertaking research on mental health problems. Professor Wilkinson is editor of the *British Journal of Psychiatry*.

DR TONY KENDRICK has been a GP for eleven years. From 1990–1994 he was Mental Health Foundation Research Fellow, and has been Senior Lecturer in General Practice and Primary Care at St George's Hospital Medical School, London since 1994. He has published several papers and book chapters on the care of people with long-term mental health problems.